The Astonishing Power of Story

Master the ultimate form of influence

Justin Cohen

Acknowledgements

Tamara Botha, Lee Cohen, Catherine Daymond, Conference Speakers International, Paul Du Toit, Ernst & Young, Famous Faces, Beth-Ann Galvin, Guest Speaker, HSBC Middle East, Nedbank World Class Service Team, Natasha John (Eskom), Donovan Marsh, Marie Grey & Associates, Richard Mulvey, Nevashnee Naicker (Sasol), Ray Mirvis, Brendan Pollecutt, Dan Poynter, Speakers Inc, Speakers of Note, Clive Simpkins.

Editor: Vanessa Perlman
Cover & Layout: Clayton Botha
Cover photo: Perfect Pixels Photography

Thank you to all of you. Either the book or the presentation is better because of you.

Contents

Prologue

20 November 1983: a nuclear weapon detonates near Interstate 70, west of Kansas City. A hundred million Americans see storms of fire annihilate the central United States, leaving a wasteland of burned-out cities, littered with the charred corpses of their fellow citizens. They hear the ghostly screams of agony from the few surviving radiation victims as the blackened skin peels off their bodies. Simultaneously the Soviet Union is attacked. It is unclear who launched the first assault. One thousand eight hundred hotlines are set up to calm terrified citizens.

Those terrified citizens hadn't suffered the *reality* of nuclear war, they had suffered the *story* of nuclear war. They had just watched a television film called The Day After. The film, a made-up tale created by writers, actors, studio sets and special effects wouldn't just require national hotlines to calm shocked viewers, it would spark peace vigils, protests and national debates. It would also go on to play a part in the real-life destruction of 2 692 weapons of mass destruction.

This book is about how stories can change the world. And when you're not too busy doing that, you'll find they're also the most powerful way to change your organisation and your life.

Once upon a time ...

Who hasn't been enthralled by those four words as they felt themselves drawn on a journey into another world? Great stories captivate like little else. They are a time machine on the wings of which we soar across the ages. Actually a time machine is too primitive a contraption to stand in as a metaphor for story. In a time machine, you still travel in your own body. In a story, you leave your body behind as you become the hero. Want to be the first king of England, the last emperor of China, Helen of Troy or how about Neil Armstrong, Lance Armstrong or Jack Welch? With the magic of story you can live all those lives and take home the greatest gift that story has to give: the lesson of a life that you didn't have to live.

Like most people, my love affair with stories started early on. There were the weekly trips to "story time" at our local library, the fat worn-out tome of children's fairy tales and fables from which my father used to read and, as far back as nursery school, the stories of the Bible. You can't measure the exact impact of a story, but there was one that probably changed my life. Like any story that deeply touches you, I really identified with the hero. To see why, you have to know what kind of child I was.

Remember those kids at school who didn't have to work hard and got an A+? I was the kid who worked really hard for my D-. In our school, if you weren't good academically, you had one other chance to redeem yourself: sport. Problem was I had the eye-hand coordination of a blind amputee. Needless to say I wasn't the happiest kid. I found my escape in day dreaming. I guess that's why some of the teachers used to call me "loskop" (Afrikaans for "loose head") or when they were in a more playful mood, "retard". We had some pretty enlightened educators back then. I'll never forget the day when the weight of my inferiority lifted. It was a Sunday afternoon at my grandfather's house. He had just got one of the first Betamax video machines. We were watching *The Secret Life of Walter Mitty*, made in the 1940s. Walter Mitty is a submissive screenwriter, talented but constantly berated by his boss, his fiancé and his mother for being a bit of a "loskop". To escape his browbeaten existence, he dips into fantastic daydreams where he becomes the heroic characters that he writes about: a fighter pilot killing Nazis, a doctor saving the life of an injured child, a cowboy defending a woman's honour. Eventually he manages to take on the courage of these imaginary characters – he breaks out of his unhappy engagement, thwarts a real-life murderer and marries the woman of his dreams.

I didn't just watch that film, I lived it. Like Walter Mitty, I too was timid and accused of being a daydreamer. Yet as I watched Walter rise out of his inferiority and use his imagination to become a great writer, I realised that there was hope for me. I started writing stories, which became a lifelong love affair with the written word, with this to date being my 10th book. I wonder if that would have happened if my grandfather had never played us that old 1940s movie.

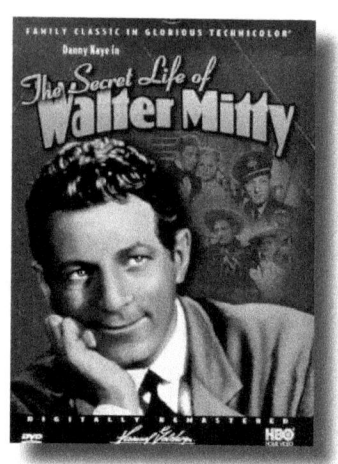

As I grew older, I became intensely curious about how stories spun their magic, how they could make you feel like you were somebody else and even change your life. Through my research both formally in my graduate studies in psychology, and informally over the past decade, I would discover that stories do way more than inspire little boys – they could change the course of human history. There are the novels and films that have altered political policy and social behaviour, but there are also the stories that set the course of civilisation for more than 1 000 years: Moses, Jesus, Mohammed. Imagine what the world would look like without any one of those storytellers. How about Churchill, Hitler and Mandela? The stories of great leaders don't just reflect reality, they create reality. Their followers live out the story, turning it into a self-fulfilling prophecy.

But stories are not just the realm of leaders and entertainers. We are all storytellers. The extent of our influence depends on the quality of the stories we tell. Even more important than the stories we tell to one another, are the ones we tell ourselves; stories about who we are, how we got here and where we're going. These stories give birth to our destiny.

Trailer

You can read this book from beginning to end or jump in where it suits you. There are five sections: a story in four acts with the final section being a special supplement on how to create your own stories to lead, sell, persuade or teach.

Act 1 is a natural history of story. We will discover how language probably first emerged and how every great epoch of human progress has been catapulted forward by the increase in our ability to tell and spread stories. You will be introduced to fascinating new discoveries in brain science that explain both the power of story and the lightning progress of humankind. By the end of this section, I think you will see that stories are our defining characteristic so much so that I propose a re-labelling of our species from *Homo sapiens* to *Homo storiens*.

In Act 2 we'll look at why stories are such a powerful form of influence and how even single words – the building blocks of stories – when flashed for less then a second, can change our behaviour. We'll discover the difference between stories and regular forms of communication and why stories are so much more likely to be remembered and acted on. We'll see how a film got hundreds of thousands of people to give away millions to philanthropic causes around the world and why 2 000 people killed themselves after reading a novel.

Every day around the world there are countless meetings and conferences with organisational leaders desperate to get their message across. In Act 3 we'll see why so many of them are failing. You will find out how stories can ramp up not just a conference but your entire corporate culture. We'll look at specific examples of what I call mission, vision and legacy stories that leaders can tell to inspire, persuade and teach. You will get a "story time" process to collect success stories that recognise exceptional individuals and spread excellence.

The lifeblood of any organisation is sales. The greatest tool in a salesperson's arsenal is a good story; you will learn how to use stories to close deals. Then we'll look at word-of-mouth stories – the majority of all buying decisions are made after hearing a story from a satisfied customer. We'll find out how to get those stories.

In Act 4 we'll look at *your* story. You will see that the difference between a depressed and a happy person is in the story they tell themselves. You will discover the kinds of stories that almost all successful people tell. But the ultimate story is told not in words, but in actions – your life is the most important story that some people will ever read. By the end of Act 4, I hope you'll be clear about what that story is.

At the end, you'll find a special supplement – a practical guide to help you create your own stories to lead, sell, persuade or teach. Here you will learn a simple six-step story-creation method that outlines the basic structure of any great story from a Hollywood movie to a two-minute anecdote. You will discover how to add sizzle to your story through humour and metaphor. But the words of a story are only half the story; the other half, is in the telling. You will find out how to tell a story with passion and conviction, how to deal with nervousness and how to make your audience "see when you speak".

Before we set off, you may have noticed that I use the word "story" to refer to all forms of communication including:

- Traditional stories that entertain educate or persuade.
- Embedded stories that define an organisation's brand and culture.
- The usually unarticulated stories we have about who we are.

Why use the word "story" to cover virtually all language? "Story" comes from the Latin meaning "account of events"[1]. In that sense almost all language is a form of storytelling. But the word "story" implies more. When we think of a story, we think of fiction. Fiction is an invention of the mind. All language has this inventing quality. That's why two people can see the same thing or event and come up with a different description. This is useful to remember when you look at your life or organisation. Whatever you find will be a story, your story of the way things are. If you don't like it, you can change it. This doesn't mean pretending you're not going bankrupt if you are. It may mean changing your story around bankruptcy. Is it the end of the world or a chance for a new beginning? It may mean changing the end of the story by changing your actions. When you look at your life, organisation or world as a story, you endow yourself with the creative power to rewrite it.

Time to get the show on the road. You're about to go on an inspirational journey back to the birth of humankind to see how the explosive speed of progress has been driven by our unique ability to tell stories.

~

The Story of Story

In the beginning was the Word.
– The Bible, John 1:1

Your caveman brain

To understand the power of story, we need to go back to the beginning. Anatomically modern human beings were born about 200 000 years ago in Africa[2]. That means, deep down inside we are all African, some of us just lost the rhythm! Imagine you were that first guy. Call him Adam. If imagining you're a black African male born 200 000 years ago feels like a stretch, it shouldn't. If you walk down the street and look into the eyes of the first stranger you encounter, you can be sure that no matter what their colour, creed or gender, you are staring into the eyes of a relative. That person is 99.9% genetically identical to you. (It's that 0.1% difference that makes you so much better looking!) In fact there are bigger differences *within* racial groups than there are *between* them.[3]

So imagine you're Adam, our first human ancestor. You roam the African savannah in a band of about 20 people, naked, without moisturising sunscreen. You forage for wild plants, scavenge for meat, sleep in a cave and die at the ripe old age of 17. Your descendants will live almost exactly like you for about 160 000 years and yet they have virtually the same brain as a human being born today.[4] Now no offence to cavemen, but what the heck were they doing for all that time?

Fortunately, around 40 000 years ago, we get off the cave couch and start doing stuff. There's the invention of sophisticated tools and shelter, the control of fire, the first interior designers get artistic on those cave walls, we start feeling like a change of scenery as we invent boats that take us around the world, there's religious belief. It's an explosion of human development sometimes called the second big bang. For a long time, there were people saying that there must have been some kind of genetic change that increased the size of our brains. But then, how do you explain the past 150 years where we've changed almost as dramatically? My grandfather used to marvel that in his lifetime he went from driving in a horse and cart to a motor car to a jet. Imagine that you died in 1850 and came back to life today. You would see beings who speak to little pet animals, against their heads (how else would you make sense of all that yapping into cellphones?) in a language you barely understand, ride inside the stomachs of great beasts at impossible speeds and sometimes even fly, not just like a bird, but fly to heaven! You would think: "Where are the humans who are these wizards?" You would have a question that up until recently we couldn't answer. How is it that virtually the same brain inside the heads of people who ran around saying: "Ugu ugu ugu" for 160 000 years is the brain that put a man on the moon.

A revolution in brain science

To crack this mystery we need to go to the University of Parma in Italy, on a hot summer's day in 1995 where a monkey is sitting with electrodes in his brain. Researchers are assessing the brain's response to movement. Whenever the monkey picks up a peanut and puts it in his mouth, certain neurons in his brain fire and the machine goes brrp brrp. At lunchtime a student walks into the laboratory with an ice cream. The monkey stares at him and then something astonishing happens: as the man raises the cone to his lips, brrp, brrp, the machine goes off. Even though the monkey sits completely still, just watching the student lift the cone to his lips makes the monkey's brain respond as if he makes the movement himself.[5] Called mirror neurons, these microscopic brain cells fire both when we observe an action and when we act ourselves. I say "we" because it was soon discovered that humans have an even more sophisticated network of mirror neurons covering several parts of the brain.

When you watch somebody walking for instance, part of your brain, your mirror neuron network, simulates the action as if it is you doing the walking. This began a revolution in brain science. See, up until then, it was thought that the brain was like a window through which we looked at the world. Now we know the brain is actually more of a virtual reality machine. To understand what other people are doing, we don't just observe, we experience it internally as if we were doing it ourselves.

You walk into an office block and a super sunny receptionist gives you a big warm smile and, almost against your will, you start smiling too. We don't just mirror actions, we mirror the emotions of the people around us. That's why negative people tend to bring us down while happy people lift us up. When volunteers lay in a brain imaging machine and watched someone smiling, their brains reacted as if they were the ones doing the smiling, only not quite to the same extent.[6] Needless to say, the same happened with a scowl. Emotion is contagious. All the more reason to choose who we hang out with. Be with who you want to be.

Ever wondered about the basis of empathy? Dr Christian Keysers found that when people watched a hand reach out to caress someone and then saw another hand abruptly push it away, the part of the brain that registers the social pain of rejection lit up.[7] We really can *feel* one another's pain. Just think of when you see someone bang their finger hard with a hammer. You wince as if the metal just came down on your own sorry thumb. That's your mirror neurons at work putting you in their shoes. You may even have felt a twinge of pain reading those words. We don't just mirror what we see, we mirror what we imagine.

Psychologist Alan Richardson took a group of basketball players and divided them into three groups. The first group practised free throws every day for 20 days. The other two groups only did a physical practice session on the first and 20th days. But members of the third group spent 20 minutes every day visualising themselves practising. At the end of the experiment, Richardson found that the group that practised every day improved 24%. The group that only practised on the first and 20th day didn't improve at all. Incredibly the visualising group, which also only did a physical practice on the first and 20th day, did 23% better – almost as well as the first group![8] No one really understood why, until now. The third group was using mirror neurons. Through the use of brain scanning, we now know that when we imagine ourselves acting, there are subtle but very real movements in the muscles that would be moving if we were physically acting. Our mirror neurons may sit in our brains, but they affect our whole bodies.

The mirror neurons explain why we love stories so much. When Superman jumps off a building and soars through the air, you don't just watch, you fly. When Keira Knightley saunters on to screen radiating charm and grace you feel yourself a little more charming and graceful. With our mirror neurons, we don't just watch or read the story, we live the story and that can change us when we go back to our own lives. Getting to spend the afternoon as Walter Mitty, I discovered that if he could rise out of his inferiority and be something more... so could I.

But the mirror neurons are more than just a virtual reality machine: they're a school where we learn just about everything we know. Although some animals have them, the sophistication of ours gives us a serious edge. Not that you'd think  so looking at a baby. By the time most animals are at the peak of their abilities we humans can barely walk or talk, we sleep for 18 hours a day and wake up every three hours screaming – whoever said they slept like a baby, obviously never had one. But our crowning achievement is when we stop defecating on ourselves, which only takes about four years. So if we come into the world so pathetic, how do we go on to become masters of the universe? Well, you see everything great an animal is, it was born with. Everything great we are, we have to learn. It's our ability to learn that has propelled our development beyond our ancestors' wildest imaginations. The most powerful learning we do, courtesy of our mirror neurons, is imitation.[9]

Human see, human do

Stick your tongue out at a dog and it will probably wag its tail. Stick your tongue out at a baby and it sticks its tongue out back at you – we may be pathetic, but we're no walkover! First we simulate the action internally with those special mirror neurons of ours, then we imitate. It's how we learn to walk, to talk, to make and sell products, to give good or bad service, to form healthy or unhealthy relationships – it's all a process of imitation. Mirror neurons see, mirror neurons do.

If you were born 100 000 years ago in a troop that ran around naked saying: "Ugu ugu ugu", so would you. You would have had the same incredible ability to imitate that you have today, you just wouldn't have had great role models – some of us still don't. It would be great to think that we create ourselves from scratch, but almost everything we are we have imitated – even our personalities.

Some psychologists believe that certain people are just born shy and stay shy.

Psychologist Robert O'Conner thought otherwise. He showed a film to a group of extremely shy pre-schoolers. In the film a solitary child watches some kids playing. Gradually the child joins in and has lots of fun. Simple story: character is alone, sees kids having fun, joins in and has fun too.

After seeing the film, or should I say *living* the film, the shy children immediately became more sociable. Even more astonishing, six weeks later, the withdrawn children who had not seen O'Connor's film remained as isolated as ever while those who had viewed it were now the most sociable in their class.[10] How did the very fabric of their personalities transform? Their mirror neurons enabled them to simulate a new reality and then imitate it. Want to know what happens when kids continually watch violence? They don't become the Dalai Lama.

When I was a kid, I thought I was dumb – when your teacher calls you retarded and you have to work really hard to get a D-, it's not a far-out conclusion. Little did I know then that I had probably just imitated poor study habits and my teacher had just imitated, I don't know, Hannibal Lecter. But even when imaginary characters like Walter Mitty helped me to rise above my perceived limitations, my early studies in psychology were still telling me I was born with them. Old-school psychology will tell you that genius too is something you're either born with or you're not. From this, there is a sad conclusion: why aspire to greatness if it's something you can't acquire? The latest research is turning this notion upside down. Anders Ericsson, a professor of psychology at Florida State University, has spent the past 20 years studying exceptional individuals in all fields. His conclusion: "Nothing shows that innate factors are necessary for expert-level mastery in most fields."[11] In fact, excellence develops by imitating and practising excellence.

I've got a friend who joined a multi-level marketing vitamin company. Problem was, she had no sales skills. But rather than say: "I'm just not a sales person", she found someone who was and sat with him as he sold the product. She videoed him and watched that video until the tape was stretched. She imitated his words, she imitated his body language, she even imitated how he positioned himself with the customer. Did she add her own flare and style? Sure, but everything she didn't know, she imitated. By the age of 29, she had two luxury homes and was driving a Porsche. Is there something you want to be better at? Think of someone who already is. Ask if you can hang out with them. Corporate mentorship programmes are a way to formalise this process.

The successful aren't just imitators, they're "adaptive imitators", they try something out; if it doesn't work, they adapt it or try something else. The key is to try something. First get it done and then get it right. You get it right by collecting feedback from the environment, from your customers, from your team members. When was the last time you asked someone to give you honest feedback about your performance? Try this: the next time someone gives you a compliment ask them if they think there is anything you can do better. If you had spinach in your teeth would you want someone to tell you? Newsflash! They're not going to, not unless you ask. We all imitate; the successful make sure they get constructive feedback, so they can adapt and imitate better.

Imitation gets a bad rap – you never see it on a list of corporate values: "Passion, Service… Imitation!" At this year's annual conference, your CEO will probably not say: "Guys, we need to imitate more!" Imitation doesn't mean mindlessly aping someone else. There is a word for really successful imitation – it's called innovation. It means finding what works and marrying it with something else that works. Farnsworth imitated a radio and a camera and came up with a television. Ray Crock imitated a restaurant and a petrol station and came up with fast food, and obesity.

Homo storiens

My vitamin sales friend was lucky to have a top sales person to model herself on. Not all of us have that opportunity. Fortunately something pretty amazing happened around 40 000 years ago – language. No longer do I need to see you to imitate you. Now all I need is to hear the story about what you did and I can do the same. In a world with language, ideas and expertise spread like wildfire. Why did it take so long for language to emerge? Well, just about any invention depends on the ability to share information. How do you share information without language? You can but it's painstakingly slow. When language arrives, our mirror neurons circulate it with viral speed and progress explodes.

If you can't hang out and imitate the great person doing what you want to do, pick up the phone and get their story. You don't know them personally? Google them or read their book. In a world with words, the secret of success is no longer a secret. To quote Isaac Newton, we achieve by "standing on the shoulders of giants". Actually, our achievements stand on the "stories of giants". Modern scientists, artists, even sportspeople are able to progress because of the knowledge of those who came before.

Every great epoch of human progress has been driven by the increase in our ability to tell or spread stories. The graph on the right shows the trajectory of human development. The dot signifies our birth around 200 000 years ago. For our first 160 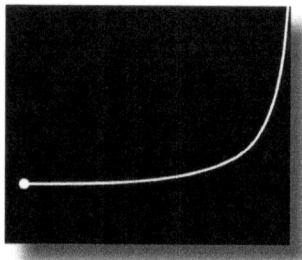 000 years we pretty much flat lined. Our development looked like a still life. Around 40 000 years ago, we get language, called the big bang of human development, the incline begins: we develop sophisticated tool use, control of fire and shelter. Approximately 6 000 years ago we learn to write; now a story can survive the death of a storyteller. We get written laws, contracts and the Bible – this is the beginning of civilisation. In 1455, we get the printing press; now stories can spread cheaply and easily leading to the Enlightenment. In the late 19th century we get film; now we can see the stories. And telephone; now we can send the stories across the planet almost at the speed of light. In the 1990s we get the World Wide Web and email. Now you can get any story, anytime, anywhere at the click of a button. When stories spread, so does progress.

Anatomically, modern human beings may have been born about 200 000 years ago, but behaviourally, modern humans began when we learnt to speak. We call ourselves *Homo sapiens*, the wise species. I'm not sure if wisdom defines us. What does define us is that we tell stories. I propose a re-labelling of our species – *Homo storiens*. (Careful who you call one of those.)

Just about every one of the great faiths puts language at the heart of human development. The Bible opens: "In the beginning was the Word." With words, we do way more than communicate, we start to think.

Imagine you had no words … How do you think about what you've done or what you're going to do when you've got no labels for that? How do you reflect on your past or plot your future? Who are you? With no way to define yourself, you're no one. You're just a collection of impulses. With language, we begin to tell a story about ourselves and the world. That's when we emerge from animal innocence.

The Old Testament Bible book of Genesis, whether you believe it literally or not, gives us startling insight into this moment. Adam and Eve eat of the Tree of Knowledge. What is knowledge, but language? They eat of the Tree of Knowledge and what is the first thing they do, go and discover the theory of relativity? No, they cover their wobbly bits. Language gives us a word for "me", now we are self-conscious. Self-conscious, we find ourselves asking deep and profound questions like: "Who am I?" "Where am I going?" and "Does my bum look big in this?" With language, Adam and Eve discover something else, something no animal knows: one day we will die. It is living with the end in sight that inspires the big question: what story am I going to leave behind?

So, to return to where we started, how is it that the same brain that ran around grunting like an ape for 160 000 years is the brain that put Neil Armstrong on the moon? The brain is like the hardware of a computer, what really makes it special is software. The software that drives human brains is stories. Our progress has been driven not by our brains, but by the stories inside our brains. That's good news. You can't get a new brain, but you can get a new story, you can find better stories to learn from, you can tell better stories to your customers and team members and you can tell better stories to yourself, which happens to be a good summary of what this book is going to help you do.

You are about to discover why stories are such a powerful form of influence and how even single words – the building blocks of stories – when flashed for less then a second can make nice people rude. We'll look at the difference between traditional stories and regular forms of communication and why stories are so much more likely to be remembered and acted on. We'll find out how a film got hundreds of thousands of people to give away millions of dollars to philanthropic causes around the world and why nearly 2 000 people killed themselves after reading a novel.

Finally, remember that story I told at the beginning, about how a Hollywood movie played a part in the real life destruction of 2 692 nuclear and conventional weapons? In Act 2, you'll find out how.

~

The Most Powerful Form of Influence

Sticks and stones may break your bones but words… can kill you.
– Justin Cohen

Word magic

If you walk down the street and see someone looking up at the sky, research shows there is an 80% chance that you too will look up.[12] Other people's behaviour influences our own even without us realising it. Our mirror neurons influence us to unconsciously imitate what we see. (Of course, we are not machines. We can deliberately choose to do otherwise, but the impulse is strong.) Now if you were to walk down the street and you heard the words: "Look up!" there is probably an even greater chance that you would. Words bypass our external senses and cut straight through to our brains, enabling our mirror neurons to simulate their meaning. They can even make nice people rude.

One group of volunteers was exposed to words that referred to impoliteness such as "rude" and "disrespectful". Another group heard words like "respectful" and "polite". They then went into a situation where they had to pass on a message to someone in the middle of a conversation. Sixty-six percent of those who had heard the words describing impoliteness butted in to interrupt, while 80% of those who had heard the words describing politeness waited the full 10 minutes for the conversation to end.[13] Unconsciously our mirror neurons compel us to imitate the meaning of the word.

Even words we don't consciously perceive can change our behaviour. Volunteers were shown an advert that portrayed four different types of rum. The phrase "U Buy" was subtly embedded in one of them. All participants said they could not detect any hidden message, yet they were 80% more likely to choose that rum.[14] You probably don't think advertising slogans work on you. Don't kid yourself. If they didn't, advertisers wouldn't be spending nearly half a trillion dollars globally every year planting messages in your brain. Sticks and stones can break your bones, but words can really move you!

Fortunately words can be used for a far greater purpose than selling rum – they can change the world. During the 2008 American presidential primary, the Clinton campaign charged that Barack Obama's candidacy was based on just eloquent words. This is how he responded:

> ... "I have a dream!" Just words. "We hold these truths to be self-evident: that all men are created equal." Just words. "We have nothing to fear, but fear itself." Just words. Just speeches ... Don't tell me words don't matter![15]

In those few sentences Barack Obama captured the power of words to transform the world. He went on to prove it, thrashing not just the powerful Clinton machine but John McCain, one of the greatest war heroes of the 20th century to become the first black president of the United States. Don't tell me words don't matter.

Listening to Obama made me think of what President John F Kennedy said to Sir Winston Churchill when presenting him with honorary American citizenship: "You mobilised the English language and sent it into battle." Churchill had great courage and intelligence but without his ability to marshal words, it is doubtful that he would have been able to marshal a nation to stand up to Hitler.

Read Churchill's words and you will see exactly what Kennedy meant.

> ... We shall defend our Island, whatever the cost may be, we shall fight on the beaches, we shall fight on the landing grounds, we shall fight in the fields and in the streets, we shall fight in the hills; we shall never surrender ... [16]

Language is truly magical. It enables us to see, hear, feel and touch without having to be there. With mere words Churchill could take his nation on a tour of their Island showing exactly what was at stake and where each needed to play their part. With his artful repetition of the word "fight" he invoked a spirit of courage and defiance. In a pre-linguistic society, Churchill would have had

to perform a war dance, shake his fists in the air and hope the troops would follow his body language – not nearly as efficient, far reaching or inspiring as a good speech. Words enable us to frame, magnify and enhance, making them potentially even more influential than direct experience.

All language is a form of storytelling in that it gives us an account of events, but there are certain kinds of stories that have far greater influence.

Stories that kill

In 1774 Johann Goethe wrote a novel called *The Sorrows of Young Werther*.[17] Virtually overnight the book turned the German author into a literary celebrity. Napoleon Bonaparte considered it one of the greatest novels and carried it on many of his campaigns. The story is about a passionate, highly sensitive artist who falls in love with a woman engaged to someone else. They become friends, but when she is finally married, he finds it intolerable. The book ends with Werther sitting at his desk with an open book, dressed in boots, a yellow vest and blue coat. He picks up a gun and shoots himself in the head.

The passionate and intellectual Werther became a powerful role model for young European men. They began to dress in boots, yellow vests and blue coats. Something else happened. As many as 2 000 young men killed themselves with a bullet to the head.

Astonishing yes, but you can begin to makes sense of this if you recall how our brains experience stories. With our mirror neurons we don't just read the book, we *live* the book. We get inside that virtual reality machine called story and experience the world of the hero almost as if we were there ourselves. When most people close the book, they go back to their own lives, but the actions, emotions and choices of the hero may continue to exert an influence. After reading about Werther, you may not kill yourself but you may be more inclined to indulge a little melancholy, or perhaps you find yourself less restrained in your

attraction to a married woman, perhaps on your next shopping trip you pick out a blue coat and boots. Quite unconsciously Werther has become a role model. It felt good to walk in his boots virtually, now you're doing it in reality.

It doesn't need to be a great literary novel; an advert can have the same effect. You see some good-looking guy wearing Calvin Klein underpants sticking out of his jeans. Your whole life you've been taught underpants go *under pants* but to continue the feeling of being Mr Cool, you unconsciously imitate his choice. Wait till Mr Cool starts wearing Calvin Klein underpants on his head.

So why didn't everyone who read *The Sorrows of Young Werther* kill themselves? For the same reason your father probably hasn't got a pair of Calvin Klein underpants sticking out of his pants. You will only imitate the "story model" if you like it and want to be like him or her. Even then, Napoleon may have admired Werther's suicide as an act of honour but it was not the right act for a man who believed his ultimate destiny was to rule Europe.

Liking and wanting to be like the character is not enough, his actions also need to make sense in your own life.

If you choose to kill yourself after reading a novel, you've got to have a serious problem. The story gives you a solution: suicide. Delivered through the attractive, romantic young Werther that solution may seem like a good one. But if you were ready for the ultimate act of self-destruction, surely you would have killed yourself at some point anyway? Apparently not.

You see the phenomenon of "suicide modelling" isn't just restricted to the 1770s. It repeats itself with almost every high profile suicide story and has been extensively studied. Award-winning suicide expert, Dr David Phillips has found that within two months after every front-page suicide report, 58 more people than usual kill themselves.[18] What is so frightening is that after the increase following the story, the suicide rate doesn't drop, it only returns to the average. These are 58 additional suicides caused by the power of a story. Even more astonishing, in the areas where the suicide has been widely publicised, there is also a significant increase in both aeroplane and car fatalities. Phillips hypothesises that to avoid the suicide label these people kill themselves in a way that makes it look like an accident.

It's not just suicide, high profile crime stories are also contagious. Stories of workplace murders produce more workplace murders – the same with school killings or aeroplane hijackings. Also known as "copy-cat" crime, this has serious implications. By reporting crime, the media may inadvertently be causing more. I wouldn't suggest that the media ignore crime, but they should be thinking more about how they report it. Given the research, they should be doing their utmost not to augment or sensationalise these stories. Reporting on the capture and punishment of criminals, as opposed to the gory details of the crime itself, may actually reduce crime, as potential criminals are forced to focus on the negative consequences of their actions.

If stories can inspire people to kill, they must also be able to inspire acts of courage and compassion. Sadly, with the media, if it bleeds, it leads, so too with Hollywood. Filmmakers like Quentin Tarantino and the Coen brothers win Oscars for films that glorify violence and nihilism. Sure, some of these films insightfully reflect reality, but they also perpetuate violence. Decades of research shows that watching violence increases aggressive behaviour.[19] That doesn't mean all films have to be Disney-style morality tales.

Changing the world

Director Nicholas Meyer was determined that his television film *The Day After*, about a nuclear bombing of America, would not become a regular Hollywood disaster film; sterilised and pretty, a teenager's boom-boom fest. Aiming for a documentary realism he insisted that there would be no American stars. He would also do everything in his power to ensure that the film would escape the censor's chopping block. Plunging himself into nuclear research for several months, Meyer was able to create a film of shocking realism. It wasn't just the fiery mushroom cloud rising above Kansas City with high speed winds of radiation flattening buildings and forests; it was the unrestrained terror of the howling victims as the skin peeled off their bodies.

Imagine watching that in the early 1980s in the midst of the Cold War. You've always known nuclear war was a possibility, for the first time you experience the reality. Just watching extracts made me feel shaky and slightly nauseous. That's because you don't just watch people scurrying like insects with nowhere to hide, with your mirror neurons you're *doing* the running. No wonder the film spurred protests, debates and peace vigils, but could it actually change an American president's mind on nuclear policy? Surely a politician with his finger on the red button wouldn't need a made-up film to bring home the horror of nuclear war?

The week nearly a hundred million Americans watched their country get "nuclear bombed", Ronald Reagan had been president for nearly three years. Afterwards he wrote in his diary, "The film left me greatly depressed … We have to do all we can to have a deterrent and see there is never a nuclear war." Long before watching *The Day After*, Reagan must have been exposed to the Pentagon's scientific analysis of nuclear warfare, he must have known about the likely loss of life and the long-term medical problems of the survivors and future generations, but all the scientific analysis in the world doesn't substitute for experiencing the reality for yourself. That's what a good story does.

In 1987, Ronald Reagan and Soviet General Secretary Mikhail Gorbachev signed the Intermediate-Range Nuclear Forces

Treaty, which would lead to the destruction of 2 692 nuclear and conventional weapons. After signing the agreement, Reagan sent a telegram to Meyer. It said: "Don't think your movie didn't have any part of this, because it did." Later Reagan would say that the film had changed his mind on America's nuclear war policy.[20] Stories don't just have to reflect destruction, they can prevent it.

Pay it Forward starring Kevin Spacey, is a film based on a book by the same name.[21] Trevor McKinney gets an assignment from his social studies teacher. "Think of an idea for world change," he says, "and put it into action." Trevor comes up with the idea of "paying it forward". He describes it to his mother and teacher like this: "I do something real good for three people. And then when they ask how they can pay it back, I say they must each *pay it forward* to three more people. So nine people get helped. Then those people have to do 27." He switches on the calculator and punches in the numbers. "Then it sort of spreads out, see, to 81. Then 243. Then 729. Then 2 187. See how big it gets?"

Trevor's idea sparks a quiet revolution with good deeds spreading through the country.

Since the book was released in January 2000, life has imitated art, a worldwide Pay it Forward social movement has emerged, with formal associations at schools and universities across the world. There is even a Pay it Forward foundation that has funded hundreds of projects supporting hospitals, schools, the elderly and homeless.[22] They have distributed nearly a quarter of a million Pay it Forward bracelets and helped spark countless acts of random kindness. Pretty good going for a story. These are not isolated examples. *The Kite Runner* is a devastating story of sexual abuse set within the horrors of Taliban-controlled Afghanistan. As a direct result of its international release, audiences paid for 70 rural libraries and the distribution of 500 laptops. *Blood Diamond* with Leonardo DiCaprio, a story about conflict diamonds, propelled a PR blitz by the diamond industry to educate consumers on conflict-free diamonds.[23]

It's not just fiction; good documentaries are also a form of storytelling that can change the world. They simply use real rather than fictional characters. We may look back at Al Gore's 2006 film *An Inconvenient Truth* on global warming as *The Day After* of climate change. The film tells two stories: one about Al Gore the defeated presidential candidate who discovers his true mission – reducing global warming. The second is about us, the earth's population and how we are killing our home. The ending is left hanging as we have to decide whether to save ourselves or be destroyed by greed. It may be a scientific documentary, but

with our planet on the brink of destruction it's also a story of *Star Trek*-like proportions. Three months after the film's release, California passed sweeping legislation to reduce greenhouse gases, it became part of the British school syllabus and hundreds of thousands of people have gone online to calculate their carbon footprint.

Sicko, Oscar award-winning documentary maker, Michael Moore's expose on the health-care crisis in the US, showed people dying from preventable causes because their medical aid refused them treatment. There is Richard, who has to decide which of his two fingers gets sewn back on because he can't afford both. The central story involves Moore taking a group of sick people on a boat to Cuba, a Third World country, where they finally get the treatment denied to them back home free. The film got some medical aids to change their rules and in the next election health-care was firmly on the agenda. *Super Size Me* is about a man who eats nothing but McDonald's for 30 days. He puts on 11 kilograms and suffers mood swings, sexual dysfunction and liver damage. McDonald's changed its menu, adding salads and ending super sizing. These films changed political and corporate policy. We can only guess how many individuals were inspired to give up their fuel-guzzling SUVs, reassess their medical aid or change their diet after seeing them.

Stories like these walk us through horror; getting sick in America with inadequate health cover, eating nothing but McDonald's, living in a world where sea levels rise by six metres. Our mirror neurons put us inside the skin of the characters and most of us will feel motivated to avoid their plight. Of course, feeling motivated and actually *doing* anything are two different things. Change depends on other factors. In the context of *The Sorrows of Young Werther* I mentioned three; whether the character's actions would make sense in your own life and whether you like and want to be like them. If you are a card-carrying Republican, you may dislike Al Gore and dismiss *An Inconvenient Truth* as self-serving Democrat propaganda.

But there are other factors, factors that govern any behavioural change. There are the perceived rewards of taking action – what do you stand to gain? There is the extent to which you think your actions will help – why do anything if you don't think it will make a difference? But there is something else. Straight after watching *The Day After* many people must have resolved to protest, write to their congressman or donate to an anti-nuclear war charity. But like a new year's resolution, come the next day, they either would have forgotten or their commitment just wouldn't seem as pressing. The story needs to be potent enough to keep you feeling motivated long after the lights have come up.

The fact that these films all effected significant change means they were powerful enough to overcome these barriers. That's at least in part because they all leverage the power of story, they don't just tell us, courtesy of our mirror neurons, they induce an experience. It's the difference between hearing that smoking causes cancer and getting lung cancer. Great stories make us feel like it's happening to us.

These are specific examples of a single story's influence, but could a storytelling industry help to build a nation?

Hollywood in Johannesburg

In the two years after I completed my degree, I backpacked around the world. My final destination was the United States. As I walked the streets of New York, I was struck by an uncanny sense that I had been there before. I just couldn't shake the feeling. It was more than a passing sensation, it was deep nostalgia. Whatever I had experienced in this city had left a hazy, wondrous, indelible impression. Finally, I got it. I had been there before! Through *Rocky* and every other movie and sitcom that

had been set in the city. From our little
Telefunken TV and downtown movie
house in Johannesburg, South Africa, I
had grown up on American stories of
love and adventure. No wonder I felt
such an affinity for the land and the
people. America was the motherland.
To go to America, was to return to the
dreams of my youth.

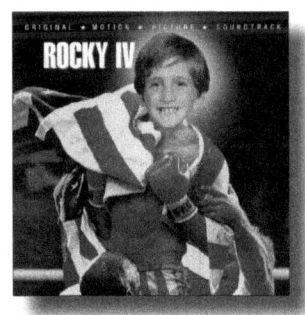

It had always struck me as absurd how some people could
protest American politics and mention their green-card
application in the same breath. Now I understood that like me,
they had America in their blood.   We had all been seduced by
American stories, hypnotised by the most sterling renditions of
the American dream. We had lived that dream again and again
through Hollywood's rose-coloured camera lenses. We had
imitated the fashions, the turn of phrase and the social mores,
we had bought the products, listened to the music and practised
the dances – remember *Footloose* and *Breakdance*? We became
so proficient, we could have starred in the sequels.

The mythologist Joseph Campbell once compared the cinema
to a temple. It engenders the same awe and reverence. We elevate
the mythological heroes and the celebrities who portray them to
minor deities. The ultimate object of our veneration is the land
where we see the dreams come true – America. No wonder the
USA is the world's most sought-after emigration destination,
attracting many of the best and brightest. According to one
20th century study, 45% of distinguished Americans were
immigrants.[24] It's these converts from around the globe who

have helped to turn the American dream into a self-fulfilling prophecy, where 300-million people have built the world's most successful economy, leading the planet in business, sport, art and science. America conquered the world not with nukes but with stories. Hollywood is her greatest advert, turning the United States of America into the secular Mecca of the world.

Life imitating art

At the time of writing, in the midst of the most severe economic crisis since the Great Depression, the idea of American supremacy may jar, but there is nothing to suggest that America won't prevail just as she has in the past. Besides, at the heart of every story there is adversity. It is adversity that transforms the man into the hero. So it is appropriate that to lead them out of the quagmire, Americans elected Barack Obama, a man who had to fight his own heroic battle – an African American, abandoned by his father, whose mother had to resort to food stamps.

In one of the most insightful statements of his presidency, George W Bush called it "a triumph of the American story". Obama's unlikely and dazzlingly swift ascent is a quintessentially American story.

One hopes that post 2009, complexion will be less of a hindrance in electoral politics, but could Obama's election be a case of life imitating art? Hollywood started electing minority presidents some time before the rest of the nation. There was Morgan Freeman in *Deep Impact*, Dennis Haysbert in the multiple Emmy award-winning series, *24*, and most recently, Jimmy Smits in *West Wing*. Smits is a Latino actor who was cast back in 2004 because of his similarity to Obama. Is it possible that the virtual reality eased America into acceptance of the real thing?

Living stories

You don't have to be a Hollywood filmmaker or a novelist to use the power of stories. All language is a form of storytelling which makes all of us storytellers. There are, however, two very different kinds of stories: dead stories and living stories. Dead stories give just the facts. Living stories may provide some facts, but they also use the traditional story elements of plot and character. They involve particular individuals engaged in specific events. A living story and a dead story may arrive at the same conclusion but they have a vastly different impact on our brains. Here is an example of a dead story:

> It is very important that even young people have a good medical aid to cover any hospital expenses that may arise. An illness may be unexpected and if a person doesn't have sufficient funds available, they may be faced with both medical and financial problems. All people should have a good medical aid.

Dead stories are often accompanied by gripping PowerPoint slides with a riveting lists of bullet points:

Now for a living story:

> My friend Howard was fit, active and just 24 years old when his doctor told him: "You've got cancer." He shook his head in disbelief, not imagining it was about to get a whole lot worse. "We need to get you into a good private hospital now, how are you going to pay?" That's when Howard put his head in his hands and started crying. As a young, healthy guy he'd just never seen the point of having a medical aid. Fortunately, after many months of treatment, he got better, but to pay his medical costs, he had to sell his flat. Four years later, he's still living with his parents.

Which of those two stories is more likely to motivate you to get medical aid? Most people will say the second one. Kicking your mirror neurons into gear, Howard's story enables you to feel the pain of not having a medical aid. That's far more motivating than a list of facts. It's the difference between Ronald Reagan hearing the Pentagon's analysis of nuclear war and seeing *The Day After*. Dead stories give you the facts, living stories give you an experience.

Living stories are specific, concrete and practical. They provide tangible events and characters. The story may be short or long, involve one character and event or many. You may even step out of the story to make a point or share some abstract facts, but it's only a story when it tells me about something that happened, be it actual or fictional.

Dead stories have their place. They are useful to create generalisations that cover a wide range of objects or events. This book is filled with abstract facts. That's because I want you to understand story as a general concept and how it can be applied to different forms of communication. To demonstrate the application of those facts, I use living stories.

The essence of living stories

You will get a detailed story-creation method in the special supplement at the end of this book. For now it is enough to know that in addition to what I've mentioned, living stories have six key components. They are always about someone (a character) who wants something – to achieve some goal. It's the **desire** for this goal that drives the story forward. There are always obstacles between the character and what he wants; this is the **adversity**. Then there is the **action** that the character takes to deal with the adversity. At some point the character will usually have some **realisation** that helps them deal with the adversity. A good story always gives us a sense of closure. It draws us to a **resolution**. He either gets what he wants or he doesn't. Finally, stories that are told to lead, teach, sell or persuade will have what I call the **take home point**, that thing that we want the audience to know or do differently after hearing the story.

In Howard's story, his **desire** is to be healthy. He faces a double **adversity**: getting sick and not being able to afford treatment. The latter, because of an **action** he failed to take – buying medical aid. Now the only action open to him is to sell his flat and move back in with his parents. The **realisation** is implicit: I should have got medical aid. The **resolution** is bittersweet; he's better but financially ruined.

The **take home point** is understood without even being stated: whatever your age, if you haven't already, make sure you get a medical aid.

The first three of these story-creation principles – desire, adversity and action – are also core to life. Desire is what drives your every action. You go to the fridge because you want to eat. You hit the sack because you want to sleep. You go to a party because you want to be entertained. Even the things you don't want to do, you do, because of some deeper desire. You cut out chocolate cake because you want to be thin. You don't buy an expensive new car because you want to retire financially independent. You stick it out at a job you hate because you want to support your family. Many desires are mutually exclusive, forcing us to choose. Whichever way you look at it we are creatures of want. The existentialist French philosopher, Jean Paul Sartre said: "The essence of life is scarcity, a universal and eternal lacking." Cheery stuff, but the man has got a point. When you say: "I want" you are saying: "I lack." If you desire something, it's because you don't have it. We spend our lives trying to fill the hole. Even when you get what you want, you soon want more or you want something else. It's like a car; you have to keep filling it up.

Between you and the fulfilment of your desire, there are always obstacles. As the American theologian Rick Warren said: "Life is a series of problems: Either you are in one now, you're just coming out of one, or you're getting ready to go into another one." If you don't have what you want, it's because there is something standing in the way. Story, like life, is largely about the action that we take to deal with the adversity. Before you contemplate slitting your wrists, think of a life without adversity. There would be no sense of accomplishment. You can't win the race without running. There is no success without struggle, no relief without danger, no satisfaction without lack.

And there are no real stories without adversity. Think about it. We spend our hard-earned free time watching TV, films and reading books where people are happy, serene, enjoying life. Not on this planet. We watch people getting murdered, mutilated, raped, robbed, fired, dumped and deceived. Why do we pay money to watch people go through the kind of adversity that we'd do anything in life to avoid? We like watching struggle because we like seeing people emerge from struggle. If the guy I just lived through for an hour can get through his adversity, maybe I can get through mine. Living stories give us hope. The really good ones help us to deal with the hardships in our own lives. They show us the actions we may be able to take to deal with our own troubles. They also remind us that heroes are forged through adversity. Life's tough and we like hearing and telling stories about it.

When you frame your information in terms of a character taking **action**, to overcome **adversity**, to satisfy their **desire**, you shine your message through the prism of our basic human condition. We are more inclined to mirror because we've hit the core of who we are. On some basic level everyone identifies with those three elements. Sure it would be easier to just fling out the facts, and sometimes that is appropriate, but if you really want your message to stick, you need to tell a story.

Living stories (which I will from now on refer to simply as stories) give us something that life doesn't: closure or **resolution**. Life is far messier. It is open-ended. Who knows exactly what will happen next? No matter how good your life is right now, tomorrow you could be a quadriplegic. With their resolution, stories give us what so eludes us in life – certainty. That might seem like cheap escapism, and sometimes it is, but great stories send us home with something else: a better way to live.

Life simulator

Stories are equipment for living.
– Kenneth Burke, literary theorist

What primarily interests me about stories is their ability to lead, teach and persuade and that's why the sixth element in my story-creation method is the **take home point**. When you tell a story, you need to be clear about what you want your audience to know or do afterwards. The power of your influence depends on the extent to which your words become their actions. The thing that most contributes to a story's behaviour changing potential is what I call "the life simulator effect".

Ever got on a plane and wondered if the pilot is a first-timer? You think to yourself: "Hey, if he's flying this Boeing 747, he must be a bright guy, read lots of books, have studied hard, passed all his exams. But what if this is his first time flying?" You remember the  first time you walked, you fell; first time you cycled, you crashed; first time you drove a car, you stalled. You don't want to be uncharitable, you know, everyone's got to have a first time, just why does it have to be with you on board!? Then you remember that documentary you saw about flight simulators. The pilot has already had his first time, he's had his 100th time in a computer simulation so real that if you were sitting in it you wouldn't know the difference. A pilot learns to fly in a flight simulator.

We learn to live in a *life simulator.* When you tell someone to give good service, it's like teaching them to fly by telling them to have a good take-off. When you tell them a story about good service, you put them inside a simulator. What makes this life simulation possible is the mirror neuron network, but there are other aspects of stories that add to their behaviour shifting power.

Getting through resistance

As I write this book, I have been looking for an example of how hearing a story changed my own behaviour. Without realising it, I have been telling that story in my keynote presentation for over a year. It's the story about Howard. Howard is based on a real person. I'd had brokers try to sell me a medical aid, but I'd always declined. Within weeks of hearing Howard's story, I called a broker and signed on. Howard didn't tell me to buy a medical aid, he didn't have to. Having walked in his shoes I figured that out myself. That's the great thing about stories, they don't tell us what to think or do. They take us on a journey in somebody else's shoes after which they allow us to draw our own conclusions. Lessons are much more powerful when we figure them out ourselves. In fact, when you try to shove a lesson down someone's throat, they'll often reject it. Why? Because!

Have you noticed, there are three ways to get something done, do it yourself, pay someone or forbid your teenagers! Well there's a teenager in every one of us. Tell us what to do and sometimes, just to assert our free will, we'll do the opposite. Psychologists call this reactance. We react to a pushy communication by ignoring it or doing the opposite even when it's in our best interest to follow it. Classic examples are when adolescents start smoking or drinking soon after being prohibited from doing so by parents and teachers. Or in *Romeo and Juliet* style, they fall more deeply in love with the person their parents oppose. Shakespeare was as great a psychologist as he was a storyteller. Researchers have found a real *Romeo and Juliet* effect. A study on 140 teenage couples found that as their parent's opposition to the relationship increased so did their romantic feelings for one another. The trend worked in the reverse, when parental resistance decreased, so did feelings of love.[25]

Stories are the best reactance busters around because they don't tell us what to do. If the story has demonstrated a convincing course of action, we will follow it of our own free will. Stories have a way of penetrating our minds without us even realising it. Imagine that instead of telling me that I really should buy a medical aid, one of those brokers had told me a Howard-style story.

Not only are stories better able to overcome resistance, when they do break through our barriers, they stick around for a whole lot longer.

Memory

If you don't read past this paragraph, by tomorrow you are unlikely to remember all the following words: young couple, road, police, A-frame roof, neatly folded clothes, safe sex.

Yet you'll probably remember a lot more than that, for a lot longer, after hearing this true story:

> In South Carolina, an hour before dawn, a taxi driver came across a **young couple,** naked and injured sprawled across the **road**. They died in hospital without regaining consciousness. **Police** were at a loss to explain what had happened. There were no witnesses, no trace of clothing, and no wrecked cars or motorcycles. Investigators eventually found a clue high on the **A-frame** roof of a nearby building: two sets of **neatly folded clothes.** The couple had gone there for privacy and accidentally fallen off. Perched on the edge of an A-frame roof is the kind of **safe sex** you want to avoid.[26]

The reason you'll now remember far more of those key words is because they are linked to a story. For thousands of years humans have remembered and passed down information from one generation to the next through stories. The best-selling book of all time is the Bible. It was written not to entertain but to provide laws for living, yet it is a collection of stories. The reason we shared our knowledge through stories rather than abstract facts has to do with the way we learn and remember.

As far back as Ancient Greece it was realised that it was easier to remember facts that were linked than those that were not. This understanding led to the creation of mnemonics – an incredibly powerful memory tool that has enabled some people to remember thousands of facts after just a single exposure.

There is no magic here. These people have just learnt to link the facts using association.

That's exactly what stories do naturally. They provide a sequence of events, each one linking to the next. These events become associated in our memory increasing our ability to recall.

To see how it works, try this experiment. Tell someone to give you 10 random words to remember. (They should give you a two-second break between each word.) Without using any technique, see how many of the words you can recall in sequence. Now try again with a new set of words except this time use each word in your imagination in a simple story. For example, let's say the first words were: toe, tree and lion. You would first picture your toe, then you might see a tree growing out of your toe and finally a lion jumping out of the tree. You will be amazed at how many words you can remember when you link them into a sequence of events like this. Even a single, stand-alone event is more likely to be remembered than an abstract fact.

Flashbulb memory

Describe where you were and what you were doing when you first heard about the 9/11 attacks. Many people can do this in great detail. Now try remembering the names of the bombers or the number of people murdered. What about the length of time from the first plane crash to the last? You would have been exposed to these facts a few times, yet you're unlikely to remember them anywhere near as well as you remember where you were and what you were doing at the time. Psychologists call this kind of long-term memory for intensely emotional events flashbulb memory. It's as if the shock of the event sears the memory into our brain.

The flashbulb phenomenon is a form of episodic memory. When you try to recall information you rely on either semantic or episodic memory.[27] We use semantic memory to recall facts such as: 9/11 was the day that Islamic terrorists flew into the World Trade Center in New York City. We use episodic memory to recall events, for example, what you were doing when you heard about the 9/11 attacks. Only highly emotional events will be remembered with the clarity of the flashbulb phenomenon, but most events (recorded with episodic memory) are better remembered than abstract facts. In fact, episodic memory is also known as "one-shot" memory because you only need one exposure to the event to remember it. In contrast, semantic memory usually requires the hard work of rote learning (unless you use a mnemonic memory tool).

Stories immerse us in specific events and so they engage our more powerful episodic memory. After hearing a good story just once, we will often remember extensive details almost as if we were remembering an experience from our own lives. Of course, if we want those stories to be singed into the brains of our listeners, they need to be emotional.

Heart over head

On 3 May 2007, while her parents were out drinking with friends, a three-year-old British girl called Madeleine McCann went missing from their apartment in a holiday resort in

Portugal. For months afterwards, the event dominated the news not just in Europe but internationally. You could watch channels like Sky and to a lesser degree CNN and feel that nothing else was going on in the world. If you drove out of Johannesburg's international airport, over 8 000km from the crime scene, you would be greeted  by a massive roadside billboard offering a reward for information leading to her recovery. (There was never any suspicion that the girl had been taken to Africa.) Madeleine's parents were invited to meet with the Pope. British MPs began wearing yellow ribbons to recognise her disappearance. Celebrities like Richard Branson made public appeals and donated over $5-million in reward money.

All this for one child. All this when around the world hundreds of children go missing daily, thousands are sexually abused or murdered and millions go to bed hungry and malnourished every night. But if all that publicity led to her safe recovery, surely it was worth it?

Early on, law enforcement officers warned that the extensive publicity was putting the girl's life in greater danger.[28] With that much international exposure, the kidnappers could not have risked keeping her alive. Yet even with nothing to report, the obsession with her story only fuelled more front-page headlines. It brings to mind the words of Joseph Stalin: "One death is a tragedy. A million deaths is a statistic." It's hard to identify with the parents of a million hungry children; it's much easier to identify with the parents of Madeleine McCann. You've seen pictures of their beautiful daughter and her parents' distraught faces; your mirror neurons have connected you with their agony, her story has become your story. Admit it, you would probably feel greater delight to know they had recovered Madeleine safe and sound than you would to hear that child abductions went down 0.8% last year. No, it's not rational, but whoever said that *Homo storiens* were rational? We are led by our emotions and emotion is the lifeblood of good stories.

The emotional memory

Think back to your most powerful memories and you will find the event steeped in emotion: your first kiss, a car accident, a family death. Numerous studies have shown that emotional memories are recalled with much greater clarity and detail than neutral events. We are wired this way to increase our chances of survival. The reason you remember the day you were mugged and assaulted as if it were yesterday is so that you are forever reminded to be more careful and avoid that part of town. The night you met the love of your life is chemically engraved into your brain to remind you that this is the person who will help you spread your genes.

In their most basic form, all emotions are variations of pain or pleasure. Anger, hatred, fear and regret are painful. Happiness, contentment, love and ecstasy are pleasurable. Pain generally tells us that something is bad and should be avoided, destroyed or changed. Pleasure usually indicates something good that should be approached, increased or maintained. (There are exceptions. Fatty foods are pleasurable because they provide sustenance and up until recently were scarce. Now their abundance has led to an obesity epidemic but we are still wired to find them pleasurable.) Usually the greater the intensity of the emotion connected to an event, the greater its survival value and the more likely it will be remembered. Stories simulate reality and so, in the same way, the more emotional the story, the more likely it will be remembered. What makes living stories intrinsically emotional is their focus on desire and adversity. Pain is our emotional response to adversity. Pleasure is our emotional response to the satisfaction of desire. When you heighten desire and adversity, you heighten emotion and therefore memorability.

Researchers showed two groups of volunteers a slide show that depicted a man and a woman on a dinner date. The couple conversed and at the end of the evening, they embraced. The story ended with the man leaving and the woman calling a friend. The difference was the one group heard an audio recording telling them that the date went reasonably well while the other group heard that the man had made some sexist remarks and the embrace at the end was an attempt to sexually assault the woman. The first story didn't contain much desire or adversity. We're not sure if the two were really interested in one another. With that story one is left with an underwhelming sense of indifference. The second story involved real desire: the man wanted the woman sexually, the woman wanted to get the hell out of there. There was also clear adversity – sexual harassment. This is what makes the second story so much more emotional.

Unsurprisingly, participants in the second group were much more likely to remember the story, but more than that, they were even more likely to remember irrelevant details like the colour of the décor or the position of the table.[29] Emotion is the glue of memory.

Studies show that even emotive words on their own, like death, sex or murder are better recalled than neutral words like beige, number or floor.[30] If you want them to remember, make sure they feel. One way to do that is to engage their senses.

See, hear, smell and touch

I was brought in to do high-level presentation skills training for a select group of business coaches. They have to do seminars to business owners justifying the importance of coaching. Of course, I encourage them to use stories. One of them came up with this story, which I have adapted:

> If you've ever climbed the jagged face of a mountain without ropes, you'll know what terror feels like. Your fingers go white as they claw on to whatever shard of rock they can find. Toes crunch into an elusive nook, supporting your whole body. You look down – woooo! The people staring up at you look like worry-faced miniatures. You turn back to the beast. A droplet of perspiration crawls down your cheek and you can smell the stink of adrenaline as your body goes into fight or flight, except all you can do is freeze, freeze and hope your aching muscles will

eventually pull you up. But they won't, not if you're a business owner. Eighty percent of businesses fail in the first five years. Right now, the majority of business owners are sprawled against that rock and they're not going to make it. The TREOC Business Coaching Academy provides the ropes you need to lean against, to hoist you to the top so you can look down knowing you weren't one of the 80% who didn't make it.

When he first told the story, I was struck by the extent to which I could see the mountain, feel the tension in my own fingers and almost smell the adrenaline. Finally, when he brought in the ropes to hoist me up, I felt the sweet relief of making it. The magic of stories is that they enable us to "speak so that they see, hear, smell and touch". That means they engage much more of our brain. The nerves dedicated to auditory processing take up just 3% of our brain's cortex. Nerves dedicated to visual processing take up 30%.[31]

Starring you

There is an old Chinese proverb: "Tell me and I'll forget, show me and I'll remember, involve me and I'll understand." Stories show and involve. My business coach client showed me the perils of running a small business without support. He could have told a more literal story, using a real-life business owner on the verge of bankruptcy who recruits the wrong people, has declining cash flow, no marketing plan and poor accounting procedures. This may have worked but it would not have applied to everyone in the audience. Too many people could have said: No, that's not me, that's not my experience of business. Ironically, by telling a story outside of business, everyone could relate. Even if you've never mountain climbed before, your mirror neurons would have taken you up that rock face and you would have linked your fear to running a business without support.

Even more than show, stories involve. We feel for at least the duration of the telling that the story is our own, although the degree of our identification will depend partly on how similar we are to the main character. The people who killed themselves after reading *The Sorrows of Young Werther* were almost all young men of a similar age and background to the protagonist. You'd be hard pressed to find a young man today who would kill himself after reading the novel because written in 1774 in a foreign cultural environment there would be much less similarity. That's not to say there wouldn't be any identification. The genius of a good story is that we can live the life of someone very different to us vicariously. It's just that similarity does increase identification.

That business coach employed a cunning technique to leapfrog over similarity and create pure identification. He told the story not from the first person point of view: "I was terrified." Not from the third person point of view: "John was terrified." He told it from the second person point of view: "You are terrified." He made us the stars of the story. Even better, the story was told in the present tense creating a sense of immediate involvement. We are not just identifying with the past experiences of a character, we are the character – now! The value of a story from any point of view is how it involves us, giving us an experience that we didn't have to live.

It's time to apply what we know about stories to boosting the performance of our organisations. You will find out how to use stories to enhance your leadership, sales and corporate culture. But right now, we're going to see how organisations waste millions of dollars boring their staff to sleep.

~

What's Your Organisation's Story?

Stories are the single most powerful weapon in a leader's arsenal.
– Prof. Howard Gardner, Harvard University

I've spoken at corporate conferences for the past 10 years. Whether it is London, New York, Johannesburg or Dubai, the routine is the same: hundreds of thousands spent on fancy hotels, guest speakers, themed dinner/dances and outdoor team builds. The objectives are to reward and recognise staff, get them networking and bonding and most important of all deliver a message that is going to enhance performance. It's that last one where they often fail. Each presenter gets up to give their State of the Corporation Address, which too often acts as a double dose

of fast acting sedatives. Perhaps you were in the audience and the presenter had just clicked on to the 40th slide, you know the one I mean, the one with about 12 bullet points and a triple bar graph that you can never quite

understand. The presenter finishes up satisfied that he's covered all the information and that's exactly what he's done – covered it – forgetting that the point is to *uncover* it.

When I suggested to one high powered executive that he do some coaching to refine his message and delivery he replied: "I'd love to, but I don't have the time." If you're a leader, what could be more important than ensuring your message becomes their mission? Like many of the company presentations I see, he made a great, big, hairy, audacious data dump, transforming into Chief Exhaustion Officer.

Fortunately this isn't always the case. I remarked to one CEO that his presentation was unusually excellent. "It should be," he said, "I started preparing it six months ago."

"Wow," I replied, "that's a long time."

"Not really," he said, "this conference is my annual sales call, a $300 000 sales call, I don't intend to waste my money." He wasn't just CEO, he was the owner.

Too many companies spend time and money on event management and nothing on message management. Without a clear message, many conferences become little more than frat parties with some all too forgettable lectures thrown in.

It's not just in the corporate world: many politicians and even more educators fall into the same trap. I went to a great university, but the vast majority of my lecturers, while experts in their fields, put little effort into the delivery of their message. I did half of my degree through a correspondence university. It was so much more productive not having to sit through droning data dumpers. You can be a genius and know your subject backwards, it means nothing if your audience is sleeping. Expertise is not enough, you've got to know how to communicate. I've found the best route to excellence is to drop the litany of dead, abstract facts and start telling stories, not just in formal presentations but anywhere that you need to sell, persuade, teach or lead.

Leadership

I was the guest speaker at an investment banker's conference in Dubai. The CEO had one main message: "Stick to your commitments. If you've made a promise to a client, follow through." Not a difficult concept to grasp, but he knew that if the team took action on that single point, service would be significantly improved. He could have simply said: "stick to your commitments" or waffled for half an hour about "our values". Instead he told a story. It went something like this:

"I was born in a village in Wales called Llangollen – don't try pronounce that with your mouth full. Population: 3 000. So what are the chances that in this room today there would be someone from my home village? Andrew, would you please stand up." Toward the back of the room a man stood up.
"I just met Andrew this morning. Andrew, tell them where you're from."
"Llangollen," he replied.
"What are the chances?" the CEO continued.
"I guess HSBC really is a melting pot. Thanks Andrew, you can sit down. Anyway, back in 1955 an unknown amateur tenor called Luciano Pavarotti

sang at our local eisteddfod and won. This event inspired him to turn professional and he made a promise that one day he would return to give a thank-you performance to the people of Llangollen. We were thrilled at the possibility, but many years passed and a lot of people began to give up any hope that he would keep his promise. This was a man who had reached international stardom and got paid millions of dollars. Why return to a tiny village in Wales? Why? Because he had made a promise. Forty years later, he came back to perform and to thank the people of Llangollen for launching his career. It was an incredible event. There were people there who remembered the day he'd arrived as an unknown in 1955. Pavarotti made a commitment and stuck to it. Do we stick to ours? Do we return all phone calls, follow through on all promises? The success of our business depends on us fulfilling our commitments. Pavarotti could do it, can we?"

You could feel the collective agreement in the room. As good stories do, it drove home a key message but achieved much more along the way. The CEO was a revered and powerful man. By telling us that he came from an insignificant little village, he disclosed his humble beginnings. Revealing vulnerability is a great way to engender empathy and build rapport. Deep down everyone feels vulnerable, we often assume those who are in power are not. We feel closer to them when we are reminded that they too have struggled and we are more likely to listen to them.

The CEO introduced us to a new member of the team, coincidentally from the same far-away village, indirectly reminding us that this was an organisation that valued diversity. Then he told a story not about banking but about opera.

He could have told a story about someone in the bank, who through much difficulty managed to keep a commitment to a client. This would have been better than an abstract definition of commitment, but keeping us in the world of banking would have been more predictable, increasing the likelihood of us switching off. By taking us into a completely different world, he grabbed our attention. There may not have been an opera fan in the room, but everyone would have known that Pavarotti (who had recently died) was the king of opera. The point would have been lost on no one: if one of the busiest and most celebrated people on the planet keeps a commitment that doesn't serve him – you don't perform in a tiny village for the money – well then, I have no excuse not to keep mine. The CEO didn't state all of this explicitly, he didn't have to, the audience figured that out for itself. This overcomes the reactance effect – something leaders frequently encounter because so much of their job is telling people what to do.

Leadership is the art of making your message their mission. To do that, most leaders focus on facts, forgetting that humans are essentially emotional creatures and are moved more by stories.

Mission story

Influence demands that you walk tall
and carry a big story.
– Annette Simmons,
author, The Story Factor

Back in the 1860s many people thought that Europeans, Asians, Arabs and Africans were like different species from different planets. It was best to keep them separated. A Scotsman called Thomas Sutherland had a different idea. He realised that we weren't that different, that a man with passion and determination from anywhere in the world could achieve just about anything, if only he had the finance to help him. One of the first globalisation gurus, Sutherland founded the Hong Kong and Shanghai Banking Corporation. Did he ever dream that his bank, HSBC, would become the largest financial group and the fourth largest corporation in the world? I don't know. What I do know is that he would be proud to see how "the world's local bank" made the world a smaller place.

When I told this story at an HSBC conference I had people come up to me afterwards asking for more information about Sutherland, who up until that point they had never heard of. They were proud of this piece of history and wanted to know more. I call this kind of organisational history a mission story, it connects staff to a higher purpose.

Most organisations have a mission statement. In South Africa, we go off on a bosberaad (meeting in the bush) and spend a couple of days figuring out our reason for being, before crafting a statement that tries to cram 14 clichéd ideas into a single grammatically tortured sentence:

OUR MISSION

To passionately provide one stop progressive and innovative products and services by offering a unique package of location, price, service and assortment through ethical and mutually interdependent partnerships with our suppliers on behalf of shareholders and the greater community to serve the varied needs of customers, synergistically.

"Huh?" When you script by committee, bad things happen. A mission statement is a mission to make and a statement that no one can ever remember! They usually have zero nutritional value for staff hungry for direction. They blabber on about "being the best" and instead make us feel bland and run-of-the-mill. Like a set of values, a mission statement is a "dead story". It usually has no sensory or emotional impact. If you can get it right it is a useful rallying cry. The secret is to make it more specific and active, even metaphorical. When Microsoft said it was going to "put a computer on every desk in every home", it turned its people into warriors, conquering the world, one desktop at a time.

A mission is the overriding goal of an organisation. It is its reason for being, its ultimate purpose. According to the Franklin

Covey Institute, less than half of US employees can identify their company's top goals.[32] It's not just that most people couldn't recite their company mission statement, who could blame them? It's that they don't actually know what the organisation is trying to achieve. Without a mission, staff are just laying bricks, how do you get passionate about that?

It reminds me of the story of two men working on a building site in the Middle Ages. A passer-by asks them: "What are you doing?" The one replies: "I'm cutting stone, it's hard, it's boring, my back is killing me!" The other replies with shining eyes as he stares at the sky: "I'm building a cathedral." Same job, better story. Better story, greater commitment.

I have a client who is one of Africa's largest clothing retailers. In the mid-90s they lost over 50% of their share price. The shareholders brought in a new executive. One of the first things these guys did was to remind their staff that they had one overriding measure of success, their share price. They put a giant digital ticker in their reception area with, you guessed it, the share price. I was always amazed at how often I'd hear staff at grass-roots level discuss why it had risen or fallen that day, or even jokingly, if somebody made a mistake, you'd hear a colleague say: "Ooh! There goes the share price." It helped that almost all staff were incentivised against the share price.

Why do we overcomplicate things and hide from the truth? If most companies were honest, they would say: "Our mission is to make more money than we made last year." I suspect that would produce more innovative products and better service than most of the mission statements out there. Not that I think this would be the best kind of mission statement, just better.

Deep down most people need to feel that they are doing more than making money. On average, money is sixth on the list of why people leave their jobs. It's that metaphorical cathedral that we want to be building.

Most leaders are managers, focussing on organising the bricklayers. Great leaders are missionaries, pointing to the sky, making us feel like heroes on a quest for the greater good. When it comes to two organisations paying the same, the one with the heroic mission wins hands down. While I encourage organisations to have mission statements (just not tedious ones), it's tough for a single statement to convey the full extent of a mission. What every organisation needs more than a mission statement is a mission story. This story provides some history about how the organisation came to be. This is not a date-by-date history textbook; rather, it tells us how we got here and where we need to go. It connects us to something bigger than ourselves.

Organisations can learn a lot from countries. A nation's history has a huge impact on its identity. Would Americans be quite so patriotic and freedom-obsessed without their revolution, civil war or segregation? Would white South African organisations willingly give away shares to their black brethren without the legacy of apartheid? Our "hi-story" binds us together and points to our future, even if that future is a contradiction of the past. In the words of Nelson Mandela in the mission story he told in his induction as president in 1994: "Never, never, never again."

Few organisations use their history to their advantage. Staff usually know little about the genesis of their companies. Maybe it's seen as irrelevant: "what got us here won't get us there."

Perhaps, but those shared memories and ideas can unite and guide us. Imagine the commitment level of the average Jew or Christian without the stories of the Bible?

When I spoke at an Ernst and Young induction programme, I put these pictures of the two founders on the screen and told this short story:

There are your founding fathers, Alwin Ernst and Arthur Young. They never actually met, although they died within days of each other, but they had much more than that in common. You see, in the early 20th century when they got into business, organisations were run like the military. Job satisfaction meant if your boss wasn't satisfied, you lost your job. Staff were 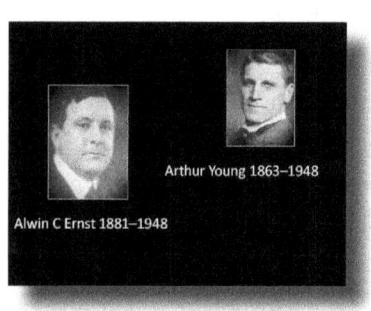 seen as expendable machines. Yet in 1920, Ernst said something extraordinary. He said: "The success of our company depends wholly upon the character, ability and industry of the men and women who make up the organisation." Round about this time, unbeknown to Ernst, Young was starting a staff school to support the professional development of his people.

Way before the management gurus of the late 20th century, Ernst and Young understood that the real value of an organisation is its people, and that education shouldn't stop when you finish university. Perhaps, it's because of that legacy that today, *Fortune* magazine calls Ernst and Young the best of the Big Four accounting firms to work for. In this week's induction and training programme you join that legacy.

Suddenly this isn't just another induction and training programme, it's living out the brave new vision of the founding fathers. The term "learning organisation" transforms from another clichéd bit of management speak into the company's collective DNA. What if your organisation doesn't have a story like that? Maybe your founding father thought people were worth their weight in mould! What if his policies nearly killed the company back in 1962? Great, tell that story. Adam and Eve made a couple of serious mistakes themselves.
We can learn from those. Besides, while your founder may have been no Gandhi, he must have done something pretty impressive to get the wheels of your company rolling. Humans hunger for meaning, purpose and mission. Feed them! Tell them a story.

A mission story connects our past to our future. Each organisation will have many. It needn't go back to the origins of the company, it could be something that happened last week. The only criteria are that it tells us something about who we are and where we are going.

Legacy story

Sasol is South Africa's largest industrial organisation. They have the highest number of PhDs of any company in the Southern Hemisphere. In the 1950s they achieved something no other company has, they perfected a process to convert coal into oil. Today the company meets 38% of the country's fuel needs. With massive hikes in the oil price, political volatility in oil producing countries and an international abundance of coal, Sasol is successfully expanding globally. You would think that creating mission stories for this company would be a piece of cake. Potential titles shout out:

"African alchemists transform coal into gold – black gold!"
"We didn't have oil so we invented it."
"Sasol: Making the impossible possible."
"Reaching new frontiers", appropriately,
Sasol's slogan.

A mission story of unbridled self-congratulation would ignore the reason Sasol managed to "reach new frontiers". Back in the1950s, South Africa was starting to be isolated because of its apartheid policies. The government realised that oil independence would be essential for its survival. Sasol was created to protect apartheid South Africa against a justifiably hostile world. You could try to sweep this bit of history under the carpet, but you would need a seriously big carpet. Sasol is still a largely white Afrikaans male organisation, (not without some self-deprecation, these guys call themselves the WAMs).

Yet the company is also transforming rapidly. Nearly half their executive is now black, they have just embarked on the biggest Black Economic Empowerment deal in South Africa's history, and many of those WAMs are transforming too. A mission story that was historically true to their past could help encourage more people to see the imperative for change.

An opportunity to tell such a story arose. One of their senior white Afrikaans executives was retiring. The company wanted to pay tribute to his 27-year contribution. Usually, this would take the form of a nice speech with a list of achievements. Instead, we created a "legacy story". This is a version of a mission story in that it connects the individual's contribution to the company's mission. When I interviewed the retiring executive to develop the story, I discovered someone who had traversed some of the most dramatic transformation in the company's history, yet also a man who had undergone tremendous internal change. I saw how his story could serve as a symbol for those who needed to embark on their own metamorphosis. The story is brutally honest about the authoritarian apartheid mentality that pervaded the early years of his career, but by the end, we see a changed man in a new organisation. If you are part of the company, watching this, you realise that the most important new frontier Sasol can help you reach is the one inside yourself. The four-minute story was played for 3 000 of the company's top leadership. By the end more than one of those WAMs was surreptitiously wiping their eyes.

The story format is audio-visual, to see it go to: **www.justinpresents.com/legacystory**.

Initially the story was only supposed to be played at a single conference, but there were so many requests for repeat viewings that it is now available on the company's intranet, used as part of training and development, and induction. Using the same format we are now creating stories to represent each of the company's values, and stories to demonstrate top leader behaviours. This is an organisation that has embraced story as a powerful culture building tool.

Inspired by my client's success, using the same audio-visual format, I started creating inspirational stories to demonstrate key success principles, applicable to most people and organisations. To see them go to **www.biglittlestories.com**.

Vision story

If you don't know where you are going,
you're going to land up somewhere else.
– Anonymous

A mission story points to our future; a vision story paints that future. It tells us exactly where we are going and how we are going to get there. This is visionary leadership, painting pictures of the invisible. You have to have tremendous faith to convincingly tell an audacious vision story. Doubt easily creeps in: "What if we can't do it? They'll think this is just pie in the sky. I'm going to have egg on my face."

One way to feel less alone is to co-opt your team into the creation of the vision. Engage in a bit of story listening and figure out where your people want to go, what they think they're capable of. One organisation I worked with got all 500 staff members to create a series of canvases depicting their view of the company's future. What emerged was a collective conviction that they have what it takes to become a top 10 global player within the next five years. These canvases are displayed in their foyer, reminding their people daily where they are headed. That's a great way to harness your people's collective intelligence and get buy-in, but it's no replacement for a leader getting in front of people and telling a story.

Some leaders struggle with vision stories because you have to talk about something that hasn't happened. Most of us are used to telling true stories about things that we've lived through. Vision stories are more like fiction, they require more imagination. In the special supplement at the end of this book you will be introduced to a comprehensive story-creation method. For now, it is enough to remember that living stories are about someone who wants something (desire), faces obstacles (adversity), takes action and finally achieves success or doesn't (resolution). Your vision story needs to contain these same elements. The heroes are the people in your organisation. What do they want? They may just want to collect a salary and go home. You need to stimulate their desire by showing them the cathedral they get to put their name on. The cathedral is a metaphor for whatever ultimate success looks like. That is your resolution: becoming number 1 in our industry, wiping out malaria, achieving a successful merger. Adversity is all the obstacles you are probably going to meet along the way. Your vision story should not gloss over these, let people know how tough it's going to be. Just make sure you provide a plan of action. Ask them for suggestions. Above all, be an optimist. Express a positive expectation that "we can do it."

When you frame your vision story in this way you get to the heart of the human condition. We all want to feel like the hero in a story, gallantly slaying dragons so that we can finally win the girl, or the top slot in after-sales service. Joseph Campbell calls this "the hero's journey". Visionary leaders show us the way.

Success stories

If you don't know the trees, you may be lost in the forest,
but if you don't know the stories, you may be lost in life.
– Siberian elder

Mission, vision and legacy stories create your corporate culture but there are also everyday success stories that can be used for recognition, learning and culture building.

Many organisations are good at recognising success, but how do you replicate it? The key is role-modelling. The most powerful learning human beings do is through imitation. Underperformers have simply imitated poor behaviour. If you want to unleash their potential, you could pair them up with your star performers. This is effective, but it only gives one person at a time the chance to learn from your stars. A better option is to get the stories about how your top performers do what they do and spread them through the organisation. This enables everyone who hears the story to emulate the star's behaviour.

Of course, it's not just the star performers who exemplify greatness. Every day in every organisation there are ordinary people doing extraordinary things. Most of these everyday heroes go unnoticed. There is a basic principle of learning: what gets rewarded gets repeated. When you tell these stories, not only are you recognising excellence, you are linking that recognition to a specific behaviour, ensuring that it happens again.

Stories are also a great way to bring corporate values alive. In most organisations, values are forgotten almost as soon as they're created. Even if they're remembered they seldom change behaviour. When staff tell stories about how they or their colleagues have lived those values, people see how they themselves can put them into action.

To get these stories, I help my clients set up "story time". Instead of spending meetings purely on policies and procedures, they start off with each person sharing a success story about how they or someone they know has lived a value, delighted a customer or in some way achieved success. You should feel the spirit in the room. It's an amazing thing: no one ever leaves an organisation because there's just too much praise and recognition. More than just recognition, each of those stories gives the rest of the team a model of excellence that they can emulate in their own lives.

Another opportunity to tell stories is award events. In many organisations when someone wins an award most people know *what* they did (increased sales by 30%), but not *how* they did it. To discover the specific behaviour of the star performers, you need to get their story and share it at the event so that everyone learns how they can do it too.

Some of my clients compile their best stories into an Organisational Bible which helps to acculturate new members of the organisation and keep established members on track. These stories become a blueprint for "the way we do things around here". Here is one story that came up at a service excellence conference. (It has been edited.)

Walking a mile in a muddy man's shoes

Something special was about to happen in a bank branch in KwaZulu-Natal. Not that you would have thought so. Sales banker Sean Bradshaw counted the minutes to closing time. His stomach growled. He had skipped lunch – again, thanks to the never-ending queue of clients. Finally, home time! He got up to go when he saw… oh, no… another client. Except this one was different. He was full of mud. Wearily Sean asked him in but nothing could prepare them for what happened next. Zulu collided with English: "Ngidinga imali ebolekisayo. Ngidinga ukukhoka ilobolo," said the man.

"I don't understand!" replied Sean. Words gave way to waving arms until finally he got it. The man wanted a loan, but he had no ID book, no proof of salary… no hope. Sean had a thought: send him across the road to another bank. It was too late, the man was coming back the next day with his ID. Sean called in a favour from a Zulu teller. He would go in armed with a translator. The next day, bombarded by the usual queue of clients, Sean had forgotten; the man had not. There he was in his muddy shoes and Sean thought: Could he not have cleaned up a bit?

"My dream," the man began through the translator, "is to marry my love, Khanyi. We are Zulu, I must pay her father lobola. I work as a gardener at a school. To get here, I have to leave work early. He glanced down apologetically at his clothes. "Khanyi's father has agreed that if I pay R4 000 as a down payment, we can get married. I have tried every other bank, they all say no. If I can't pay, I will lose her and then…" He trailed off.

That's when something happened to Sean. He caught a flash of the love in his life and he thought of losing her. The mountain was high. Mr Ntuli didn't have a bank account, he was paid in cash and he wasn't paid much. Sean phoned the school where he worked and made an urgent appointment with the principal. Inviting Mr Ntuli into his car, they sped off. Walking into the principal's office, Sean thought of what it must have taken Mr Ntuli to walk through the steel and glass entrance to the bank.

The principal agreed to all the necessary paperwork. The loan was granted and handed over to a proud son-in-law to be. The dream … was no longer a dream. Three years later the couple are happily married and expecting their first child whom they promise to name Sean Bradshaw Ntuli, after their banker.

Before you decide how to treat someone,
imagine you were them.
– Justin Cohen

No lecture on empathy, cultural diversity or "going the extra mile" could have achieved what that story did and yet, other than the quote at the end (to crystallise a key take home point), it didn't contain a single instruction.

This was one of many great stories that had conference delegates laughing, crying and above all experiencing great service in that virtual reality machine called story. This story wasn't even voted the best but because of its particular focus, management asked us to make it into a video clip. This got distributed to all 25 000 retail staff. (**to see it, go to www. justinpresents.com/successstory**)

Lately the company has set up discussion groups where staff discuss the lessons in the story and compare it to their own service successes and failures. The learning here is phenomenal. Staff aren't being lectured, they're using the story to reflect on their own experiences and discover their own insights. Best of all, knowing that they will need to share success stories at the next meeting motivates people to go out and live them.

In a famous experiment conducted in the 1920s researchers set out to test the effects of lighting on work performance.[33] Every time illumination increased, so did performance. But they soon discovered an unexpected effect. When lighting decreased, performance also improved. From this, we have one of the greatest insights into organisational psychology: with increased monitoring and attention, there will almost always be an increase in performance. It's not the intervention, it's the attention. By rewarding people for finding great stories, they begin monitoring one another, which on its own improves performance.

Our corporate culture depends on the stories we tell one another. Our profitability depends on the stories we tell our customers.

Sales

Before they buy your product,
they have to buy your story.
– Justin Cohen

A travel agent is trying to sell a package holiday to a client. The client is price sensitive and finally admits that she thinks she may be able to find a better deal over the Internet. The travel agent tells the client this story:

I had a lady who'd been booking her holidays with me for years until she suddenly stopped. I called her. She told me she was skipping her holiday. I wasn't convinced, but I let it go. The following year she came back and confessed that she'd actually gone to the States and decided to book the whole thing over the Internet.

She said booking each hotel, flight and tour was harder work than she expected, but she was happy to be saving a few thousand rand.

"So why not do it yourself this year?" I asked.

"Because," she replied "it was the worst holiday of my life. On the Internet the hotel had advertised a view. Well, the windows were so small and high up, it felt like the view from a prison cell, except a prison cell would have been bigger, this was like a walk-in closet. The speakers on the tour bus were broken, so we couldn't hear what the guide was saying; and we missed our flight to Los Angeles because for some reason my credit card wasn't debited even though I got an email confirmation."

Her list of travails continued. I asked her how much she paid. You can imagine how thrilled she was when I told her that had she booked with us, she actually would have saved money because of the bulk discounts we get. Needless to say, this year she's leaving the hard work to us. You're welcome to call her if you want to hear more about her holiday.

The sales consultant who told this story came from a company that was increasingly losing business to the Internet. If a consultant suspected that a client was considering booking over the Internet, they would tell them booking through an agent was easier and often cheaper but it wasn't stemming the tide. I asked the team to find a true story of someone who had booked on the Internet and failed to get what they wanted. Now the whole team tells this story. Most of the time, the client is convinced.

Sales people tend to just focus on the facts, spouting out lists of features and benefits. If they get an objection, they may try to contradict it with another fact. Yet as social creatures, we are concerned less with facts and more with what other people are doing. Psychologists call this social proof.[34] If it worked for you, I assume it will work for me. If it didn't work for you, I'm unlikely to want to try it myself. Tell me a success story about someone who used your product or a failure story about someone who didn't and I'm much more likely to buy. I encourage the sales teams I work with to collect and share stories. In some cases, they even script them to get the wording just right.

The great thing about stories is that they don't *push* you to buy, which usually produces the reactance effect (doing the opposite). Instead they let you walk in the shoes of someone who has used the product (or hasn't), and then they allow you to make your own decision. As a colleague of mine likes to say: "Do you like to be sold or do you like to buy things?" Nobody likes being pushed into a sale, nobody wakes up on a Saturday morning and says: "Honey, let's go be sold." What we all enjoy is buying things. The greatest weapon in a sales person's arsenal is a good story.

Estimates vary, but most studies suggest over half of all buying decisions are made after hearing a story from a satisfied customer. When you tell your client a success story, you are bringing that happy customer into the room. Of course, most of the time you don't have to bring your customer into the room, they're out there on the street talking about you to people you don't even know. The stories they tell determine the success of your business.

Word-of-mouth stories

A friend of mine arrived back from a business trip in Cape Town with this story:

> You got to try out this hotel I stayed at. It's called Extreme Hotel. Everything about it is extreme: as you walk in there're these massive chandeliers hoisted to the ceiling with climbing rope; the one lift is decked out as a diver's cage with sharks bashing their noses

through the bars; the other makes you feel like you're in a cable car going up Table Mountain; and the toilets are all themed differently: one is called Stage Fright, the whole bathroom is painted with an audience! And the smoking area is called the Coff'n Room – get it? Coughing/coffin room. You sit on a big white leather-topped coffin, you look up and the ceiling is painted with all these people crying into your grave.

My next trip to Cape Town, did I stay at Extreme Hotel? Hell yes! That story enticed me more than any advertising campaign could have. I've now recommended the hotel to thousands of people through my presentations and many more through this book. The story was based on something that really sets Extreme Hotel a part – its decor. If every hotel looked like Extreme Hotel, there would be no story. We are built to notice the extraordinary and ignore the familiar. It's a survival mechanism. If we gave our full attention to everything, we would exhaust ourselves. So the more we are exposed to a stimulus, the less we respond to it. Psychologists call this habituation.

In an increasingly commodified world, there are no stories because most products look like clones. Why should I tell you a story about something you've seen a hundred times before? So, if the guys down the road are selling pretty much the same thing that I sell, the question I need to be asking is: how can I stand out? Often that happens when something goes wrong...

I haven't told you about my LG laptop have I? I bought it because they're really great PCs. Rubbish! Like all of us, I bought the story: LG, Life's good: I love that story. And they advertise with this

handsome guy in a pin-striped suit who I want to be like. Problem was just about every day the laptop would just shut down, whatever I was working on – gone. I took it in four times but they couldn't fix the problem. Eventually I said:

"Guys, please I need you to replace the computer."

"Sorry," they said "it's too near to the end of your guarantee."

"But the guarantee's still valid?" I asked.

"Yes, but it's too near the end."

Huh? What my guarantee just entered old age, so it can't do the things it used to? Life's good? No, life's gone. Work gone, guarantee gone, laptop gone – thrown off high-rise building.

That's the kind of story you don't want your customers telling.

About a year later, LG called and gave me a sequel to the story that I now also tell my corporate audiences:

... so the lady says "I'm from LG" and I'm thinking they've got wind of my story and want to make amends, or sue me. But I soon feel like I've entered an episode of *The Goons*:

"So Mr Cohen, how are you enjoying your LG laptop?"

"You're joking, right?"

Once I realise she's deadly serious I proceed to tell her my story. I even mention that I tell thousands of people this story every year. Throughout I'm polite, emphasising that I know it's not her fault. I even make it clear that I am sure LG often provide great service but with me, they failed.

"OK, thank you," she replies, "Goodbye."

I look around the room wondering if I am on *Candid Camera*. Then I figure it out. This is after-repair service. Call the client a year later to make sure everything is OK and to show them that you care. If everything isn't OK, don't worry, it's the thought that counts.

As I go on to tell my audiences, I really don't like dissing a company. I'm sure that LG produce many great products and often provide great service. We all mess up at times. The problem is that's when our customers start telling stories about us. It reminds me of the story of the boy who doesn't say a word until he's eight years old. Doctors, psychiatrists, speech therapists – they all try to help, but can't. Finally, one lunchtime, he looks up and speaks his first words: "The soup is cold!" His mother is amazed. "I didn't know you could talk!" she says. "Why haven't you spoken before?" "I don't know," the boy replies, "I guess everything's been great up until now!"

We usually only talk when the soup is cold. We're more likely to talk about negative service experiences than positive ones.

The problem is who we talk to. Research shows that only 6% of shoppers will report negative service experiences to the store while 31% will tell friends and family.[35] And that can have a serious impact on your business. Nearly half of over a thousand shoppers surveyed said they had avoided a store because of hearing a negative story about it. Interestingly, the negative service experience has an even greater impact on those who were told the story than those who experienced it firsthand. That's probably because the teller usually embellishes the story to give it greater shock value. Remember we *Homo storiens* look out for a good story and good stories involve adversity. Companies can turn that to their advantage.

Imagine LG had replaced the laptop – even after the fifth time I'd brought it in, and sent me a handwritten note of apology along with a R50 voucher for any other LG product. They would have sold an extra product, kept me as a life-long customer and I would've had the best kind of story to tell, one with a happy ending, one that would've won them a whole lot more LG customers. You can mess up, just give them a happy ending. That turns them into marketing storytellers for you.

Advertising is also storytelling. Problem is advertisers are ranked as only slightly more honest then used-car salesmen.[36] (No offence to advertisers or used-car salesmen most of whom I'm sure are honest, but that is the perception.) We don't want to hear from the guy whom you pay to say how great you are – your advertising agency. We want to hear from the guy who pays you – your client. The majority of all buying decisions are made after hearing a story from a satisfied customer.[37]

Here is a simple recipe to get great stories:

1) Be great. There's no replacement for excellence.
2) Get the stories. When you've been great, ask for a written testimonial from your happy customers.
3) Tell the stories. Keep the stories alive. Send them to prospective customers. Put them on your website. Finally, go back to step one. When you're great, they'll be telling the stories for you.

Story reader

In the 1960 American presidential election, Richard Nixon was widely expected to beat John F Kennedy. He had just finished a successful eight-year run as vice-president with a hugely popular president and war hero Dwight D Eisenhower. Kennedy was young, inexperienced and Catholic – what many considered at the time to be an unwinnable combination. The debates were supposed to put the nail in the coffin of Kennedy's aspirations. If you were listening on radio that's probably what you would have thought. Listeners awarded Nixon a victory. Yet the larger television audience thought Kennedy had won. How did that happen given that the TV and radio audience heard the exact same thing? They may have heard the same thing, but what they saw was very different. Kennedy looked tanned, fit and well rested. Nixon was wearing an ill-fitting shirt and having turned down make-up, he was sweating under the hot lights. Worst of all, his five-o-clock shadow made him look shifty.

It's not just the story *you tell* that counts, it's the story that people read into how you dress, look and speak. Sometimes the story they tell about you is better than reality (better looking people are usually thought to be more intelligent);[38] sometimes it's worse (people with heavier accents are thought to be less intelligent).[39] We aren't just storytellers, we are story readers and even when you don't tell us a story, we'll find one about you to tell ourselves. It's the way we make sense of the world, find meaning and spend our money.

What do a Porsche Cayenne and a VW Touareg have in common? Well let's see, they have the same chassis, similar shape, engine, many of the same components, they're built from the same blueprint in the same factory. Oh, apparently there is a difference: the VW handles steep slopes better. I'm sorry, I forgot, there is one more difference: the Porsche is more than double the price. Why would anyone pay more than double the price for the same car? Why? Because we don't buy a car, we buy a story.

When you drive a Porsche, the story is: I am rich, young and sexy. Even if you're 80, impotent and the bank owns the car. We don't buy what we need, we buy what we want and what we want is a particular kind of story.

Champagne and Cap Classique are both sparkling wines made in the same way: the one in France, the other in South

Africa. My favourite Cap Classique is called Pongrácz – it costs about $9. My favourite champagne is Moët & Chandon – it costs $45. In a blind taste test I did with friends, most people couldn't tell the difference. In fact, not realising she was drinking the Cap Classique, one woman remarked: "You can tell this is champagne, it's so much better." The crazy thing is, I can't tell the difference, yet I still buy both. Why? Because when I see a bottle of champagne, a story runs through my head, a story that goes back to my childhood when I discovered that this was the most expensive, luxurious drink in the world, made far, far away in the beautiful French countryside, so special that you didn't call it wine, you called it "champaaagne".

That's a pretty good story, good stories are good marketing because we don't buy products, we buy stories. For a long time, I did feel a little duped until I discovered this study by Antonio Rangel of the California Institute of Technology.[40] He found that when volunteers were told that the wine they were drinking cost $5 a bottle, the medial orbitofrontal cortice of the brain, where we register pleasant experiences, didn't register much activity. Later, they were given the exact same wine but told that it was a different wine costing $90 a bottle. This time the pleasure centre of their brain lit up like a Christmas tree. That means that although most people can't tell the difference between Moët and Pongrácz, when they see the difference in the bottle and price, the story they tell themselves increases their physiological pleasure. Stories are not just perception, they are reality.

Your offices, promotions, packaging and products all tell a story. You want to control that story because that determines whether they buy and how much they'll pay.

Harvard researchers placed two sets of identical towels in a home furnishing store. The one set of towels carried a logo: Fair and Square.

Attached was this message:

> These towels have been made under fair labour conditions, in a safe and healthy working environment which is free of discrimination, and where management has committed to respecting the rights and dignity of workers.

The other set had no such label. Not only did sales increase when they carried this message, they kept increasing as the price was raised.[41] Same towel, different story. Your profitability depends on the power of your story.

Now that we've looked at your organisational story, it's time to look at your personal story. You will see how the only difference between a happy successful person and a depressed failure is the story they tell themselves. We'll look at the most important story of all – the story you will leave behind. But how does changing your story change your life? You're about to find out.

~

What's Your Personal Story?

Your story gives birth to your destiny.
– Justin Cohen

David worked in the frozen food distribution business as a packer. You couldn't fault his work. He arrived on time, kept the refrigerators neatly stacked and always finished up by 4.30pm. He did everything his job demanded. That was the problem. If he was asked to do anything else, he would look sullen and make up an excuse to get out of it. One day his manager, Barry, sat him down: "David, you've been here four years, you're a bright guy, you could be promoted. Instead you're probably going to get fired."

David looked confused: "I always do my job."

"Do you want to get ahead?"

David shrugged.

"Do more than your job." Barry indicated that the meeting was over.

David got up but hovered at the door.

"What's it?" Barry asked.

"Sir, my father was a farm hand, he worked like a dog, sometimes the farmer wouldn't even pay him. I was 13 when I promised myself I was one black man who wouldn't be anyone's slave."

Barry got up and leaned forward on the table: "You don't work hard for me. You do it for you. In this world that's the way you rise above slavery."

The next day David arrived on time, finished earlier than usual and that's when he did something he had never done before – he asked admin if they could use an extra hand. By the end of the year, he got a promotion. The following year he moved his kids to the best school in the neighbourhood.

This story came out at one of my corporate success story workshops. I had become a little sceptical about the possibility of instant change, but here it was. A man had turned his life around after a single conversation. Look a little deeper and you see that something fundamental had shifted; his personal story around work. Before the conversation you could summarise his story as:

"Your boss will try to take as much as he can from you for as little as possible. To be a free man you need to make sure you do no more than you have to. Fail in that and you become a slave like your father."

After the conversation it changes to:

"There are good managers who may want to help you. To be a successful man and give your family a better life, you need to work harder than you have to."

Everyone has a story about who they are and how life works. For most people, that story is unarticulated, but it still guides their actions. Someone who exploits others at every opportunity has a story of a dog-eat-dog world where you need to take as much as you can before someone else takes from you. Most depressed people have a story about a harsh world where they are at the mercy of whatever happens. We all have a story that underlies our beliefs and behaviour. David's childhood as the son of a farm hand with an exploitative boss, clearly set him up with a story where authority is to be distrusted and extra work avoided. Yet two people can go through the same adverse circumstances and emerge with a different story. That may have something to do with having a manager in your life who takes the time to suggest a new one.

When I fail at something, at the back of my mind I can still sometimes detect the old defeatist story that used to dominate my childhood: "Face it, you're just not clever enough." Struggling to get through school and having a teacher call you retarded creates fertile ground for that sort of personal story. When I catch myself, I change it: "It's not what I was born with, but what I do with it that determines my destiny." Our minds are a bit like a radio with many stations, each broadcasting a different story.

We need to make sure we are tuned into the right one. How do you figure out the story that's currently dominating your life? Listen.

The constant storyteller

Those who do not have power over the story that dominates their lives, the power to retell it, rethink it, deconstruct it, joke about it, and change it as times change, truly are powerless, because they cannot think new thoughts.
– Sir Salman Rushdie, author

Stop reading for 30 seconds, close your eyes and take note of what you hear.

. . .What did you hear? The sound of your breathing? Traffic? You also would have heard a voice, the thinking of your mind. That's right, you don't have to be psychotic to hear voices in your head! That voice is your internal storyteller. We are constantly telling stories to ourselves. A story is just an interpretation of reality, there are many stories you can tell about the same thing. But there are two main types, for example:

> At the time of writing, I've sent this book to three different publishers and they've all turned it down. Obviously this is just not a mainstream book. No one was ever going to take it. The moment one person says no, the rest are probably going to do the same. I hate it, but there's nothing you can do about it.

That's what we call a **pessimistic** story. Let's take the same event but tell a different story:

> At the time of writing, I've sent this book to three different publishers and they've all turned it down. I've got about 200 more to send it to! I'm confident that eventually it will be published. I may need to get some constructive feedback and change a few things. Perhaps I'll go the self-publishing route, but one way or another, I'll get this book out.

That's what we call an **optimistic** story. Same event, two different stories. We don't get depressed about life, we get depressed about our story about life. When depressed people are taught to tell more optimistic stories, they reduce their depression more effectively in the long term than with anti-depressants.[42] Compare brain scans of those who have had a course of anti-depressants and those who have learnt to become more optimistic and you will see similar shifts in the action of serotonin – the brain's happy chemical. Change your story and you change the chemistry of your brain.

Whether you are an optimistic or pessimistic storyteller is so critical to your success because of the nature of life. Just as stories in books and films are essentially about people overcoming obstacles to satisfy their desires, life contains one obstacle after another. Your personal story around those obstacles determines your eventual success or failure. The defining characteristic of a pessimist is low expectation. Not believing that the obstacle is surmountable he doesn't take action and proves that it isn't.

If the pessimist had a motto, it would be: "Things are going to get a lot worse … before they get worse." In story terms the pessimist looks forward to a sad ending. A life of depression and defeat is almost always connected to a pessimistic story, while the successful will almost always have an optimistic one. You may think that the optimistic storyteller is optimistic because good things have happened to her, while the pessimist tells those downbeat stories because he has had a spate of bad luck. No doubt, what happens to us does influence the story we tell, but the connection is far lower than you would think.

In 1989, two professional speakers had an idea for a book. They would compile an anthology of true inspirational stories. Driven by a calling that "you can change the world one story at a time", they spent three years finding the right title and format and collecting the very best inspirational stories. Finally, it was ready to be published. They sent it to 33 of New York's top publishing houses. These were the comments they got back: "We don't think there is a market for this book", "We just don't get it", "It's not topical enough", "It's too positive." They continued sending it out. All totalled they were rejected by 140 publishers. To top it off, their agent said: "I can't sell this book – I'm giving it back to you."[43] At that point, most people would have assumed they had a dud and given up. Fortunately, they were optimistic storytellers. Read their books, and you'll see what I mean. So they kept at it and eventually found a lesser-known publisher who was willing to take a chance. Good thing they kept at it or Jack Canfield and Mark Victor Hansen's *Chicken Soup for the Soul* would not have sold over 110 million copies to become one of the bestselling book franchises of all time. Was being an optimist enough to achieve success? No, they had to be willing to work hard and deal with rejection, but had they not believed success would eventually be theirs, they would never have put the work in. How many people with projects greater than *Chicken Soup for the Soul* will we never hear of because after the third rejection they told themselves the story: "You may as well give up, it will never happen."

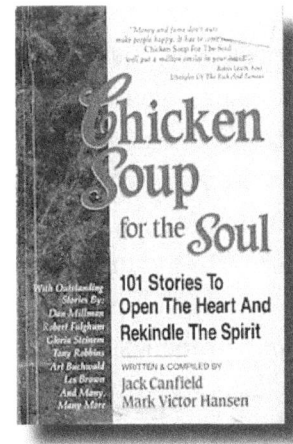

Just in case you think Canfield and Hansen's book was an unusual case, JK Rowling's Harry Potter series was turned down by 12 publishers. Imagine after the 10th rejection she had said: "Enough is enough, it's time to go back to waitressing." Well, for one thing, she wouldn't be richer than the Queen of England. More importantly, the world would have lost out on the gift of her imagination and millions fewer kids would be reading. Most great endeavours fail many times before they finally succeed. Both pessimistic and optimistic storytellers get knocked down, it's just that the optimist gets back up. Why? Because the optimist believes that eventually, she will prevail. She takes positive action because she believes in a happy ending.

We can all be pessimistic storytellers at times, particularly when we are faced with adversity. There are two questions you can use to shift from a bitter to a better story. No 1: "**What is good about this?**" For every loss, there is a gain. If nothing else there is a lesson, as the Dalai Lama says: "When you lose, don't lose the lesson." According to Tulane University business professor, Lisa Amos, entrepreneurs fail in an average of 3.8 business ventures before they finally make it. Failure is the best teacher in town, if you're prepared to be instructed.

Perhaps you're thinking: "You don't know what's going on in my life right now, there is nothing good about this." Well, see how your story compares to Alison's. A few years ago, I interviewed her on my television show. Alison was abducted, gang-raped, stabbed and disembowelled. Finally her throat was slashed 16 times and she was left for dead. The doctors called her survival a miracle. She told me something I will never forget, she said: "Even if I could, I would not choose for that night to unhappen". The experience had helped to build her courage and tenacity. Not only had she become a hero to people around the world, in her own words: "I appreciate life more because I have had this trauma." Alison discovered good in the most abject evil. Does this make what happened to her good? Of course not, but it does demonstrate that for every loss, there is a gain – if – and this is the crux of it – we allow ourselves to find it. Had Alison kept telling herself the story: "This isn't fair, people are evil, I will never get over this," she would not have recovered, written a book, become an inspirational speaker and helped so many other people deal with their trauma.

The second story changing question is: "**What can I do about this?**" Don't underestimate the power of that question. When you start telling stories about solutions, you will break through just about any problem. If you're really struggling, write down five solutions. You only need one, but the way to get one good solution is to get lots of possible solutions.

Our stories don't just live in our heads, they live in our conversation. Have you noticed that a pessimistic storyteller can light up a room just by walking out of it! An optimistic storyteller is not naïve, she knows "shift happens", but nothing grows without manure. What kind of storyteller are you?

Mission story

The stories we read in books and see in films are always about a character taking action to achieve some goal. This reminds us that goal orientation is central to life. Your goals give you meaning, they are the focus of your life story. You will have many goals, but what is your overriding mission? To figure that out look at the difference you are making in the world. What is your contribution? Or, if you are not yet contributing, what would you like your contribution to be, what fills you with passion? At the end of your life, if Hollywood made a movie about you, what would you want it to look like?

My mission is to inspire people to realise their potential. Ideally, it's something I live on a daily basis. It manifests in many ways; through my writing, speaking, coaching and consulting. I find it particularly useful to reflect on my mission when I'm wondering how to spend my time. If the activity is not in accord with my mission, I know I should probably not do it. At other times, I may not like the activity but when I reflect that it serves my mission, I feel better about it.

At my presentations, I hand out what I call a wrist reminder. It's a black band stamped with the words: "What's your story?" Wearing one reminds me to be conscious of my story, to see whether I'm living it through my thoughts, words or actions and if not, to change it. If I find myself telling a negative, pessimistic story I may ask myself: "What is good about this?" or "What can I do about it?" A colleague of mine, one of South Africa's top film directors tells me this little physical reminder has had a profound impact on his life. Whenever he sees or feels it, he reflects on whether he is living his mission to make great movies. If he finds himself slacking off, the bracelet motivates him to take action that better serves his calling.

Once you know your mission, the question is: "What would the ultimate realisation of my mission be?" You need to paint a picture of success, something that you can see, feel and believe in. In story terms, this is your ultimate resolution. Of course, there is likely to be adversity along the way; the obstacles that hinder you. The "hero's journey" is never without struggle and so you need to carefully plot out your path. You need a goal achievement programme, (you can get one by going to www. justinpresents.com). Of course, you can't anticipate all the obstacles, but the better your map, the better your chances of getting there.

Most of us are better at telling stories about what has happened than what is going to happen. Perhaps it's the fear of disappointment. If I create an audacious vision story I may be setting myself up for failure. Know upfront, that not everything you envisage will come to pass. I have had grand visions that have not materialised, but at least if you know where you want to go, you give yourself a chance of getting there. Some people don't want to be locked into a vision because they fear their desire may change. That's true and that's why you need to regularly update your vision. Businesses that start out with no clear plan are significantly less likely to be in business five years later than those who do.[44] The interesting thing is, five years later those with the plan are usually following a different plan, often moving towards a different vision. It's the clarity of focus that is critical even if that focus changes along the way.

When it comes to achieving that vision, or anything in life, I have found the two most prevalent stories are: "I can" and "I can't" stories. Whenever you find yourself saying: "I can't because … I'm too old, too young, male, female, black, white, uneducated, dumb, inexperienced. I can't because of the government, the economy, the breast milk supplement my mother fed me …" you are moving towards a dangerous self-fulfilling prophecy. Sure, you need to know what's holding you back so you can deal with it, but most "Why I can't" stories are simply reasons for not doing anything. It's the story that too many of my white South African brothers who say they can't get a job because of the colour of their skin tell themselves. (Well over 60% of management in South Africa is still white and the country has a serious skills shortage.) As long as you believe you can't do something because of something that is outside of your control (skin colour, gender, innate intelligence), you will never try. Believe you can't, you won't. Is there something you want to achieve? Try writing an "I can" story. Write down five reasons why you can: list your talents, abilities, social support and knowledge. Know this: there are people with less talent, intelligence and resources than you who are achieving more. It comes down to what Henry Ford said: "You think you can, you think you can't, you're always right." Change your story and you change your life.

Your mission story is focussed on the future, there is also the story you tell about the present. That story has the greatest impact on your happiness.

Gratitude story

Who is rich? He who rejoices in his portion.
– The Talmud

I worked on a rural development project in Nieu Bethesda, a town of 800 people in the Karoo desert of the Eastern Cape of South Africa. This was during apartheid. The black community had been granted few amenities. The only real opportunity was to be a domestic worker or farm labourer. There was a 70% unemployment rate. Yet laughter, singing and even dancing in the dirt and dust of the sand streets of the township was common. The people seemed happier than many of those I encountered in the affluent white suburbs of Johannesburg. I couldn't really understand why, until I found myself standing high on a grassy mountain outcrop with a small group of youths from the Xhosa tribe. As we looked out into the vast, majestic mountains of the Karoo, one of the young men began to shout out prayers of gratitude into a great big clear blue sky. The wind howled about his incantation. As others began to shout their praise, we spontaneously raised our arms in reverence to the universe. And then, just as suddenly, there was silence, nothing but the haunting hollow tones of the wind. We walked home quiet and content, with a deep appreciation for life. You don't need to be a millionaire to be rich; you just need to celebrate the bounty of what you already have.

Most of us are pretty good at telling stories about what is wrong with our lives, what we don't have, what should be different. It is important to acknowledge what needs to change, but for our emotional wellbeing it is even more important to appreciate what we have. Studies show that happy people are grateful people.[45] It's not what you've got, it's your appreciation of what you've got that makes you happy. Continuously focus on what you don't have and you'll feel deprived and depressed. Focus on what you do have, and you'll feel rich and happy. Having a mission with clear goals doesn't mean disregarding the present. The climber who only enjoys himself once he gets to the top of Mount Everest has just sacrificed a year of training and climbing for five minutes – that doesn't seem like a great trade. The moment of achievement is just a moment, the joy is in the journey.

I have a simple gratitude story that I tell myself that immediately raises my emotional state. I simply focus on whatever is happening in the present moment and tell myself what I love about it. I do it when I go running or early in the morning before getting out of bed but any time is good.

To give you an idea of how it works, I'm going to do it right now as I sit in bed, writing this book on my laptop:

- I love the breath rushing through my lungs.
- I love the smooth white column on the balcony outside.
- I love that big bushy blue-grey tree.
- I love the feel of my body pressed on the mattress.
- I love the rich red of the couch.
- I love that I'm 35, fit and healthy.
- I love my friends.

- I love Tamara.
- I love life.
- I love that I can love.

The words "I love" immediately programmes us into a different state. By fixing that state to something specific in the moment or in your life in general, you straight away raise your appreciation and happiness. The world reflects our internal reality. If you go through life with an "I hate story", you're not going to have much fun.

The story you leave behind

After reading a book, it's easy to feel that your work is complete but no athlete ever won a gold medal after finishing a book on running. It's what he put into practice afterwards that made the difference. I hope you've enjoyed this story, but the most important stories are told not in words but in actions.

Here is what you can do to improve your story:

- Find somebody great to imitate or read their biography.
- Practise adaptive imitation and request feedback.
- Set up "story time" where you tell success stories about yesterday and vision stories about tomorrow.
- The next time you have to sell, lead, persuade or teach, try telling a living story, (further guidelines in the last section).
- Dream up ways to give your customers a more memorable story.
- Get clear about your personal vision story.

- When life hits the fan ask: "What is good about this?" and "What can I do about it?"
- Replace "I can't" with "I can" stories.

Above all, live out a story that you would be proud to have told about you. Your life is the most important story some people will ever read – certainly your kids. But take consolation from one of my teachers who told me: "It doesn't look like you can be a good example, so you'll just have to serve as a terrible warning!"

The ultimate story is the one we leave behind. It was a Sunday morning, I was four years old when my brother mentioned in passing:

"When we die …"
"What?" I said, "I'm not going to die." I don't know how I thought I'd do it – like maybe have myself preserved in syrup. I ran to my dad:
"Daddy, I'm not going to die am I?"
My father looked down at me. "We all die,"
(he had a great way with kids)
"… but not for a long, long time."
"But one day?" I asked.
"Yes."

That Sunday, I cried until I was too exhausted to cry anymore. I wasn't to be consoled by thoughts of an afterlife – who wants to be a ghost? All I knew was that Justin Cohen would die. But that same day, a seed of a question was sown, one that I put to you: At the end of your life, what story will you leave behind? Whatever is happening in your life now, the next act is in your hands.

Our journey has come to an end. The special supplement that follows is for those of you who are looking for a method to create your own stories to lead, sell, persuade or teach. You will learn a simple six-step story-creation process that outlines the basic structure of any great story from a Hollywood movie to a two-minute anecdote. You'll find out how to use humour and metaphor to enhance any story. But the words of a story are only "half the story", the other half is in the telling. You will find out how to tell a story with passion and conviction, how to deal with nervousness and how to make your audience "see when you speak".

~

Special Supplement
How To Tell Better Stories

To be a person is to have a story to tell.
– Karen Blixen, author, Out of Africa

Telling stories is like wearing clothes, everyone does it, some just do it better than others. Simply telling a story does not ensure better communication. It would be better not to tell a story than to tell a long and boring story. Reminds me of what a farmer friend of mine said about one of his colleagues: "Johan has a special talent for making a short story long."

By following some basic guidelines you can make sure you get the most out of your story. The essential ingredients of stories are events and people, or to use story language; plot and character. We're looking at the use of stories for the purposes of learning and persuasion so the most important question in constructing your story is: what do I want my audience to know or do differently after hearing my story? I call this the **take home point**. The problem with most of the corporate presenters I see is that they try to tell the audience everything they know, which is like throwing the proverbial spaghetti at the wall and hoping some of it sticks. The average audience suffers from an epidemic of Attention Deficit Disorder. You're lucky if they remember and act on one thing. Once you're clear about what that one thing is, start thinking about examples from your own life, other people's lives, the news or even fiction that demonstrates the point. Once you've selected the best one, you can begin to follow the **DART** story method.

Desire
Adversity & **A**ction
Realisation and **R**esolution
Take Home Point

D – Desire

In all stories, there needs to be someone who wants something. If the character is likeable, the greater his or her desire, the greater the disappointment we'll feel when they don't get what they want or the satisfaction we'll feel when they do. The more intense the emotions we feel while listening to the story, the more likely we are to remember it.

> **Key question**
> Who is the main character and what does he or she want?

A – Adversity

A story is not a story without some struggle. Something needs to get in the way of our characters achieving what they want. What is the obstacle, the setback, the barrier to success? Adversity could look like some external danger, but it may actually be some internal character flaw. You build **suspense** by creating uncertainty about whether the adversity will be overcome.

> **Key question**
> What stands in the way of the main character getting what she or he wants?

A – Action

Another word for the events of a story is the action. The specific action I want to highlight is what your character does in response to the adversity. This is where the learning is. If the action works, you've got a success insight that your audience can imitate in their lives. If the action doesn't work, they also learn something – what *not* to do.

> **Key question**
> What does the character do to deal with the adversity?

R – Realisation

The action that the character takes to deal with the adversity may emerge out of a realisation that he has. Alternatively, after taking action, he may have a realisation. This usually relates to the key lesson of the story.

> **Key question**
> What does the character realise?

R – Resolution

There are few things as unsatisfying as a story without an ending. The resolution answers the big question: Does the character win or lose? Do they overcome or succumb to the adversity? Great stories will often take us by **surprise**. Just as we think the hero is going to succeed, he fails or if the ending is happy, just as we think he is going to fail, he succeeds.

Key question
How does the story end?

T – Take Home Point

What is the key lesson of the story? The wisdom of a great story provides many lessons and different lessons to different people. Still, as the storyteller, you need to know what the main one is. Sometimes your take home point will come out so clearly through the telling of the story that you won't need to state it. But if you really want to be sure that they've got it, you may want to state it along with a question that helps the audience or reader to apply it to their own lives.

Key question
What do you want the audience to know or do after hearing your story?

The nuts and bolts

While the DART method gets to the essence of story, here are the nuts and bolts to put it together.

Setup

It is usually best to start off the story by introducing the main character or setting up the time or location. This eases the audience in, getting them into a receptive, story-listening mode. Kids' stories do this with the phrase: Once upon a time. The moment a child hears those words he knows he's in for a treat. Probably not the phrase to use with your business colleagues; rather let the specifics of your story dictate the opening. Occasionally, to increase surprise and impact, you could start a story by getting straight to the heart of it: "There was a loud explosion ..." But even then, to avoid confusion you will soon have to tell us where we are and who is involved.

Detail

Giving the audience a little detail about what the environment or characters look like helps them to picture it. Detail also adds authenticity, increasing the sense that this actually happened. When you tell me your Grade 1 teacher Mrs Draklin wore her grey hair pulled back into a bun making her face look like a half-peeled onion, you paint a compelling picture. The detail should help to drive the story, accentuating the desire, adversity or resolution. If Mrs Draklin was the villain of the story, that description would enhance the adversity. Don't get carried away, too much detail and you've got the perfect remedy for insomnia.

Dialogue

"Don't do it!" I screamed.

Compare that to: "I screamed at him not to do it."

Letting the characters speak for themselves helps them to come alive. Dialogue creates immediacy by driving the audience right into the moment.

Turning point

What keeps stories interesting is how they contradict our expectations. Like a good joke, the ending comes as a surprise. More than the ending, throughout the story there are mini turns of fortune. After a streak of winning, the main character begins to lose or after seeming to succumb to adversity, he begins to triumph. In short anecdotes there may only be one turning point at the end, which brings us to our final story principle.

Surprising but inevitable

The biggest surprise should come towards the end. As surprising as it is, it also needs to be believable. More than believable, it should feel as if it couldn't have ended any other way; it was inevitable. Think of watching a great thriller: when the true killer is revealed you are surprised, but it makes perfect sense. You may wonder why you never figured it out earlier. Not all stories have to be that surprising, but if it's predictable, it's boring.

Humour and metaphor
These are optional, but as you will see later, they are a great way to increase the impact of any communication.

Story sample

I'm going to demonstrate some of these principles by analysing the final story that I told at the end of Act 4.

I was looking for a story that would demonstrate the following lesson or **take home point**: "Death can come at any moment, you will live on in the story you leave behind. Make sure you live out a story that you would be proud to have told about you." Looking for personal events around death, I remembered one of the most powerful incidents of my early childhood, the day I discovered that humans die. I was devastated because for the first time I realised I was not going to live forever. That's really all that happened, but by linking this event to my take home point, it becomes a profound lesson.

Applying the DART method, my **Desire** is to live forever. The **Adversity** is death. The **Action** is running to my father. **Realisation, Resolution** and **Take home point** are condensed in the final line.

Let's analyse the story line by line.

> *It was a Sunday morning, I was about three years old when my brother mentioned in passing, "when we die…"*

This **sets up** the story providing a visual context.

"What?" I said, "I'm not going to die."

Here **dialogue** helps my little four-year-old self come alive, particularly when I add a subtle change of body language, vocal tone and facial expression.

> *I don't know how I thought I'd do it — like maybe have myself preserved in syrup.*

This story deals with a weighty issue. Bringing in a moment of **humour** helps to lighten it up without trivialising it.

> *I ran to my dad: "Daddy, I'm not going to die am I?"*

In the act of running to my father, we see my desperate **desire** not to believe in the hard reality of death.

> *My father looked down at me. "We all die."*

The finality of his words accentuates the **adversity**.

> *He had a great way with kids.*

Another moment of humour to lighten the load.

> *"… but not for a long, long time."*
> *"But one day?" I asked.*
> *"Yes."*

Again, to accentuate the **adversity**, the reality of death is not candy-coated.

That Sunday, I cried until I was too exhausted to cry anymore. I wasn't to be consoled by thoughts of an afterlife – who wants to be a ghost? All I knew was that Justin Cohen would die.

This first **realisation** deepens the **adversity** and adds a moment of humour.

But that same day the seed of a question was sown, one that I put to you: At the end of your life, what story will you leave behind?

Notice that the actual event as it happened didn't really have a resolution. If you want to know what happened, the next day I went to nursery school and told some of my friends who I was surprised to discover already knew about death, and I gradually learnt to accept it. That's not much of an ending. Instead, I created a **resolution** out of a **realisation**. "… That same day the seed of a question was sown, one that I put to you: At the end of your life what story will you leave behind?" The adversity is dealt with through the realisation. In this story, **realisation, resolution** and **take home point** are one. The great thing about stories is their flexibility, you can jump forward in space and time, cutting out the extraneous and condensing the pertinent.

Don't let the story-creation principles bog you down. As you start creating your story, rather focus on what happened. As you edit, you can apply the principles to improve the story.

From DART to DARTING

Only half the story is the words, the other half is how we tell it. We create the story with DART, here's how to tell it so that it goes DART**ING** into the hearts and minds of each and every member of your audience.

I – Imagine
The best way to take an audience on a journey is to go with them. Don't just say the words; imagine them for yourself. To make the audience feel, you need to feel yourself. Relive the pictures, sounds and above all, the emotions you or your characters felt at the time. The better you imagine the story for yourself, the better the audience will experience it.

N – Non-verbally communicate
A story is told not just with words but with facial expressions, tone of voice and body language. Some studies show non-verbal communication to have even more impact than verbal. Just try telling someone you love them with folded arms and a scowl on your face.

G – Give the story to your audience
Most people get nervous telling their story because they're scared of being judged. They become self-conscious as they focus on how they sound or look. Well, here's the thing: it's not about you, it's about the audience. Take the focus off yourself and focus on what you passionately want your audience to understand or do differently. Think about how they will be better off after listening to you. Give them the gift of your story.

Metaphor

Metaphors are instant stories: In a single word or phrase you can immediately transport your audience into another world. We all use metaphors every day. A metaphor or simile compares the thing you want to communicate to something more sensory and emotive or just better able to highlight your point. (A simile uses the words "like" or "as" to make the comparison – "She looks like a goddess." A metaphor simply substitutes one for the other as if they were the same thing – "She *is* a goddess.")

Another example of a metaphor: let's say someone was really indecisive and you wanted to inspire them to act. You could say: "You need to make a decision." Or using a metaphor you might say: "Grab the bull by the horns!" The word "grab" converts the intangible, internal act of making a decision into something sensory and physical. This engages not just our brains but our bodies. Courtesy of our mirror neurons, the word "grab" may well produce some subtle stimulation in our finger muscles as we internally mirror the act of grabbing. The picture of a bull conjures up challenge, strength, and excitement. Grabbing those horns suggests courage, even heroism. Which is more inspiring: the heroic act of grabbing a bull by the horns or being instructed to make a decision? What may have been a mundane decision just turned into the excitement of a rodeo. Just look back over this paragraph. It took nearly six lines to explain what that metaphor said in six words. And those six lines don't have nearly the impact of that brief phrase.

A metaphor like "grab the bull by the horns" is a cliché because it has become such a well-known phrase. Despite what your English teacher said, there is nothing wrong with using a good cliché that properly illustrates your point. Where she is correct is that it won't be as effective as something fresh that people haven't heard before. The more you hear something, the more your brain ignores it. Here is how you can create your own metaphor to suit any occasion.

The **TILE** metaphor method:

- **T**ake home point — What do you want your audience to know or do?
- **I**t's like ... what can your point be compared to?
- **L**ink the metaphor back to your point.
- **E**dit the phrase so that it is as brief as possible.

Let's apply the method.
I worked with trainers of a property investment course. After a seminar describing the value of the course, they often have to deal with people who are keen to sign up but still procrastinating. They were looking for a metaphor that would inspire them to act. This is how we applied the TILE metaphor method.

Take home point
You've assessed everything, now you need to make a decision and sign up.

It's like ... (Compare it to something else)

- Diving into a cold swimming pool. At first it's cold, but as soon as you start swimming, you warm up.
- Choosing from a menu. If you don't make up your mind, you're going to go home hungry.
- Your car. Until you start the ignition, you're not going anywhere.

We chose the third example because the image of the car carries the most power and excitement.

Link

The car is a metaphor for the property investment course. We wanted to convey that this was the best property investment course, so we made the car a Ferrari.

Edit

After playing around with the words, this is what we came up with:

> You're sitting in the Ferrari of all property investment courses. But you can't just sit there. You've got to start the ignition. Are you ready to accelerate yourself to financial freedom? It's as simple as signing here.

You can use a metaphor to make any point, to describe your product or service, overcome an objection or close a deal. The key is to know what you want to communicate and compare it to something more visual and exciting, or just to be better able to make your point. I was working with a pharmaceutical company. They had a new drug for diabetes called Diamicron. The sales representatives were experiencing resistance from the doctors because the drug was unfamiliar. Yet those same doctors were very comfortable prescribing another of the company's drugs, Coversyl, for hypertension. Why? Because Coversyl was familiar and had a track record. To the doctors, Coversyl was the gold standard for high hypertension. The reps wanted to convey the fact that Diamicron would soon become the gold standard for diabetes. Like Coversyl, it was safer than many of the competing drugs, it had been researched extensively and was highly effective. We were playing around with metaphors that the reps could use to convey this to the doctors. Eventually one of them said: "Diamicron is the Coversyl of diabetes." In this simple metaphor, the new drug gets to borrow all the positive qualities of the old, making the unfamiliar, familiar.

We use metaphors all the time, often without realising it. Do you know what a "live memory-staging area is"? It's where your emails are stored. So some bright spark said, let's just call it an "inbox". How about "a structured user interaction table"? Using another metaphor, that's what we call our "desktop".[46] Translated into old fashioned but familiar office features, these complex technological breakthroughs become familiar and accessible. (Talking about office features, that's what Microsoft metaphorically called their software – "Office"). Find yourself trying to explain something that people just aren't getting? Look for a metaphor.

Humour

Adding humour to a story can really liven it up. In the speaking community, we have a joke, a newbie speaker asks an established pro: "Should you use humour in a presentation?" The pro replies: "Only if you want to get paid." As we saw earlier, even and perhaps especially with a serious subject like death, humour is a great asset.

I had a television show on which I interviewed experts on success. One of our most popular shows was my interview with Victor Vermeulen, a brilliant speaker and author who is also a quadriplegic. Victor was destined to play for the national cricket team when he broke his neck in a diving accident. Below his neck, he is completely immobile. He shares some powerful life lessons but what strikes you is how he peppers his stories of struggle with humour. Here is one of the stories he tells:

> I met former president Nelson Mandela. Like a lot of people, he made the mistake of offering a handshake when we met. I told him I couldn't shake his hand, not because I'm a racist ... but because I'm totally paralysed. He laughed and then told me he would pray for a full recovery.

Humour prevents Victor's presentation from lapsing into self-pity or melancholy. It puts the audience at ease. Those feel-good moments of laughter make us more receptive to hearing about what it takes to live each day in the face of such adversity.

But the purpose of humour is not just to lighten up heavy subjects. One of the biggest challenges with any presentation is that the audience has to sit still for a long period of time. Prolonged stillness generally leads to sleep or irritation. Laughter transports fresh flows of oxygen into the brain, enhancing attention. According to Dr William Fry, 100 to 200 laughs a day is the equivalent of about 10 minutes of jogging.[47] Now I wouldn't substitute a workout to sit in front of the cartoon channel, but if you want to wake up an audience, get them laughing. Even better, laughter boosts endorphins, the pain-killing chemicals that produce feelings of wellbeing. When you use humour, those good feelings become associated with you and your message.

When it comes to using humour, avoid telling a joke that has nothing to do with your content. The best presenters are able to link humour to enhance or even make a point. Google the subject you want to find a funny remark for along with the word "joke" or "humour". There are loads of humour sites with funny lines on just about everything. Be sure to adapt the joke to fit in with your story. You can also create your own humour. By flexing your humour muscle you will find yourself better able to come up with spontaneous, off-the-cuff comments, but even the best comedians prepare most of their humour.

I am now going to describe a formula for creating humour. This applies to a stand-alone funny line or one that forms part of a story. We'll dissect some funny lines to see how the formula works. Unfortunately a joke is like a frog, when you start dissecting, you kill it. When you know a joke is coming and you are looking for the mechanics, the humour dies. Also much of the impact of the joke comes through your delivery. My point: these jokes are probably not going to split your pants, but there is much you can learn from them.

Structure of humour

There are two key phases to any joke: the **setup** and the **punch line**. The setup raises certain expectations and the punch line draws us to a surprising conclusion that trashes those expectations.

Take this joke for instance:

> *My wife and I have only ever*
> *had one argument, it was*
> *soon after we married...*
> *30 years later, it hasn't ended.*

The setup is the first line. It gets us thinking along a certain train of thought, this guy has only had one argument with his wife, wow, they must have a great marriage. The punch line is a total **surprise** because it is the opposite of what the setup was leading us towards. It **contradicts** the setup. Often this happens by a **change of meaning**. In the setup, we interpret one argument as being in one place and time. In the punch line, the words change to mean something that is continuous. And in this case it is of course an **exaggeration**. No one argues *that* much. Humour also **ridicules,** which is why it can so easily offend. The joke mocks both husband and wife. It could be softened with another funny line such as: *"How do you think we've stayed so passionate all this time? The make-up sex is fantastic."* Again, **surprise**, the last thing we were thinking of these guys doing was having passionate sex and it's also a little **ridiculous** that you have to have a fight to make love. Because ridicule is such a big part of comedy, the safest humour is directed at ourselves or someone who is strong and confident enough not to mind a little mockery, unless you want to ridicule a competing service, product or even idea. Ultimately humour highlights a certain **truth**. The joke reminds us of a sad fact: many couples spend a lot of their relationship arguing.

There is a seventh element of humour not evident in this joke, **comparison**. This is metaphorical humour where you compare one thing to another:

The perfect speech is like the perfect skirt...
long enough to cover the essentials,
short enough to keep the interest.

This old joke makes an important point (truth) by comparing speech making to something frivolous (ridicule).

So to summarise, there are seven elements of humour, three of which are essential:

1. Surprise (essential)
2. Ridicule (essential)
3. Truth (essential)
4. Contradiction
5. Change of meaning
6. Exaggeration
7. Comparison

Let's apply the elements to create a joke. Say you are promoting a valuable but pricey product or service and you want to gently ridicule a price objection. Ask yourself what is ridiculous about price objections.

- In the long run, buying cheap is often more expensive.
- Focusing on what something costs at the expense of what it does.
- Not realising that cost and benefit go hand in hand.

The **setup** needs to have us believe that decisions based on price are good, the **punch line** needs to **surprisingly contradict** that view.

Want to know the best part about
buying really cheap?
When it breaks, it's really cheap
to buy a new one.

The first line is the setup. The second line **surprisingly changes the meaning** of "really cheap" implying that having to buy a new one, makes it really expensive.

I always say: buy on price ...
If you want to say bye to quality.

The setup suggests that buying on price is a good thing. By playing on the word "buy", the punch line produces a **surprising change of meaning**. This is a classic pun, when the same sounding word can mean two different things.

Want to pay less for more? Easy,
pay less... for more trouble.

The **setup** suggests you can pay less and get more value. The **punch line contradicts** our expectation – **changing the meaning** of "more" so that it refers not to value but to problems.

Not all of these jokes would be appropriate all the time. Remember that because the joke ridicules, you can come across as an irritating smart aleck. A good way to reduce any possible offence would be to make the joke about yourself, what we call self-deprecating humour. So you could say:

I'm a thrifty guy, I always wanted to pay
less and get more. Then I realised that's
exactly what I got, I paid less and I got
more... trouble!

The joke has the same impact but instead of mocking your client's price sensitivity you're mocking your own. They can make the connection to themselves without you shoving it in their face.

Comic timing

"Ask me why I can't tell a good joke"
"Okay, why can't you..."
"Timing."

You can create a really clever piece of humour, but if you don't deliver it with the right rhythm and pause it can be as funny as bread mould. When you listen to comedians or sitcoms, become aware of how timing increases the humour. A simple rule is to pause between the setup and the punch line. If you go back to the jokes I created above, you will see that I put an ellipsis (three dots) after the setup. This is to signify a pause. Remember the setup gets us thinking in a particular direction by pausing afterwards to let the meaning sink in. After that pause, you want to come in fairly quick and punchy. That's why it's called a "punch line" – you need to punch out the words so it hits them in the face, unexpectedly. Remember, humour comes through the unexpected shift of meaning from setup to punch line. Your pause and change of rhythm highlights the contrast.

Creating a story

Using humour and metaphor, let's apply the DART method to create a story. I wanted to tell a story to my corporate audiences to demonstrate service excellence. Starting with my **take home point,** this is what I wanted them to know and do.

> You will often have to deal with difficult or even rude customers but you can choose whether to allow yourself to be infected with their negativity. Even better, sometimes by changing your own response, you may be able to change theirs.

To clarify the take home point, you might ask: "What do I want my audience to do differently after hearing this story?" I would answer:

> *The next time they encounter a rude customer, I want them to choose to stay positive and in the process change their customer's emotional state.*

At this point, I started to think about incidents in my life where I was in a negative state and someone's positive response changed the way I felt.

> At my father's funeral, most people greeted me with sadness and awkwardness. In contrast, my uncle put his arm around me and gave me a warm, supportive smile. I immediately felt my spirit lighten.

The story would also work the other way round: I could be

the one who changed somebody else's emotional state. For example:

> *As a teenager I was in love with an older girl. We were good friends but she had made it pretty clear she didn't have any romantic interest in me. This made me feel down around her decreasing my attractiveness. One day, instead of moping around her I resolved to be upbeat and confident and finally to ask her to kiss me. It worked!*

Although neither of these story possibilities are directly about customer service they make my point which I could easily bridge over with a final statement such as:

> If you don't like your customer's response, change your own.

Still, neither story was working, they felt too far removed. I was going to be talking to service personnel and I wanted them to immediately see the application. I started reflecting on my own customer interaction experiences. I remembered an incident that had happened some months before:

> I had gone to visit a client at a big insurance company. The receptionist was downcast and abrupt. I felt myself getting irritated. At that moment I had a thought: I'm not going to let this lady affect my state. I gave her a big smile and she smiled back!

Applying the DART principles, this is how I clarified the story elements.

Desire
I am the main character in this story. What I want is a positive interaction.

Adversity
The adversity seemed to be the unpleasant receptionist, but actually it was an internal character flaw – my allowing her to bring me down.

Action
The action that changes everything is my smiling at her.

Realisation
That action emerged from a realisation: I get to choose my emotional state.

Resolution
By changing my own state and action, I changed hers – ultimately getting what I wanted: a positive interaction.

To develop my stories, I like to write them, but in my story-creation workshops, delegates are paired up so that they can create their stories through dialogue. What works when you write it down doesn't always work spoken out loud. It's in the telling that you realise certain phrasing is more effective, or you find ways to increase the desire or adversity, or the impact of your take home point. So even though I start off writing my stories, they change as I tell them.

This is how I currently tell the story:

I went to visit a client, one of South Africa's largest insurance companies in their big, beautiful, shiny headquarters in Johannesburg. Entering the triple-volume foyer makes you feel like a king. Except, I quickly felt like a pauper. You see, when I got to the front desk, the receptionist barely looked up to acknowledge my presence. When she did, she looked at me kind of like a side dish that she hadn't ordered. You know that look. (*I demonstrate.*) It reminded me of the waiter who left his job to become a traffic cop. He said: "The pay and the hours are terrible, but at least the customer is always wrong!"

So after giving me the "side dish" look, what do you think I did? I did what any self-respecting man would do. I gave her the "side dish" look right back! As if somehow that would teach her to be friendlier. As I did this, I thought of Gandhi's words. OK, I didn't really think of Gandhi's words, that's kind of a motivational speaker thing to say: "In that moment Gandhi's words came into my head!" But the sentiment of Gandhi's words did come to me: Create the change in yourself that you want to see in the world. There and then I resolved to choose a better state.

After notifying my client that I'd arrived, I noticed her nametag, gave her a big smile and said: "Thanks so much, Sandy." What do you know, Sandy looked up ... and smiled. Emotion is contagious. The best way to protect ourselves against other people's negativity is to realise that nobody can make us feel bad without our permission. If you don't like your customer's emotional state, change your own.

Let's analyse it:

I went to visit a client, one of South Africa's largest insurance companies in their big, beautiful, shiny headquarters in Johannesburg. Entering the triple-volume foyer makes you feel like a king. Except, I quickly felt like a pauper.

I **set up** the story by describing the location. A little bit of **detail** is important so that it feels real. I obviously didn't want to reveal the name of the company but by placing it in Johannesburg and describing the interior, I achieved the same thing. The detail you provide should serve the story. By describing the grandeur of the interior, I made it clear that I felt good and was expecting (and **desiring**) to continue feeling that way. I could have said: "You walk in and the triple-volume foyer makes you feel really good." By saying "... makes you feel like a king", I used a simile, (similar to a **metaphor**) which magnifies just how good I felt. That set up our first **surprising turnaround**: "I quickly felt like a pauper."

This re-emphasised my driving desire to feel good.

> You see when I got to the front desk, the receptionist barely looked up to acknowledge my presence. When she did, she looked at me kind of like a side dish that she hadn't ordered. You know that look. *(I demonstrate.)*

The **adversity** was her sour face. To bring in humour, I looked up "insults" in my subject indexed book of jokes. It was something Ring Lardner Jr had said after meeting with President William Taft: "He looked at me like a side dish that he hadn't ordered." This is a classic use of **comparison** in humour. You compare the thing you want to **ridicule** to something derogatory. I was being looked at like something inhuman — a misplaced side dish! I adapted this joke to the story (storytellers have got to be magpies!) and added some physical humour by demonstrating her look (**non-verbal communication**) which always gets a great laugh. Remember, it's not just the story, it's the telling.

> She reminded me of the waiter who left his job to become a traffic cop. He said: "The pay and the hours are terrible, but at least the customer is always wrong!"

This was another joke I adapted from something I found on the Internet, which makes my point and gets me a great laugh. It uses **comparison**: I compare Sandy to a traffic cop. The joke itself **contradicts** our expectation that the customer is always right and **ridicules** anyone who actually operates in this way, providing a great lesson all on its own.

> So after giving me the side dish look, what do you think I did? I did what any self-respecting man would do, I gave her the side dish look right back. As if somehow that would teach her to be friendlier!

This **action** deepens the **adversity**. I am obviously making the situation worse. That's the great thing about stories, they show us which actions work and which don't. In fact, we are realising now that the real adversity is not her so much as my action, which shows my **character flaw**. What I also like about this is that it shows me in the wrong. While you are telling a story, you are the leader. We like to see our leaders as humble and honest, not know-it-all braggarts.

> As I did this I thought of Gandhi's words. OK, I didn't really think of Gandhi's words, that's kind of a motivational speaker thing to say: "In that moment Gandhi's words came into my head!" But the sentiment of Gandhi's words did come to me: "Create the change in yourself that you want to see in the world."

When I first used to tell the story, I would use Gandhi's words as my **realisation**. This was taking a little too much poetic licence.

I had not actually thought of Gandhi's words at the time, although I was familiar with what he'd said and certainly I was driven by the sentiment. One day on the spur of the moment I came clean with the audience and told them I hadn't actually thought of Gandhi's words and took the opportunity for some self-deprecating humour, mocking my profession, the motivational speaker. The audience was in hysterics. I decided to permanently incorporate the line. The challenge is to make it feel as spontaneous each time round. The way to do that is to **imagine** that I really am coming up with it on the spur of the moment.

> There and then I resolved to choose a better state. After she had notified my client that I'd arrived, I noticed her nametag, gave her a big smile and said: "Thanks so much, Sandy." What do you know, Sandy looked up and… smiled.

I **resolve** the **adversity** by changing my **action**, which leads to a **surprising and inevitable** result; the abrupt and downcast Sandy smiles. The three dots signify a pause, which increases the impact of the **turnaround** and even though it's not a particularly funny line, with the right pause, people usually laugh.

> Emotion is contagious. The best way to protect ourselves against other people's negativity is to realise that nobody can make us feel bad without our permission. If you don't like your customer's emotional state, change your own.

This final piece is my main **take home point.** The story may make the point on its own, but these final lines re-emphasize it, increasing the likelihood that it will be understood and acted on. On a side point, some of you may notice that the second last sentence is an adaptation of something Eleanor Roosevelt once said: "Nobody can make you feel inferior without your consent". I think I've changed the words sufficiently not to have to officially credit her. There's that magpie again.

Now, go and build your story, metaphor and humour muscles and lift your communication to new heights!

~

[1] Ayto, J. (1990). Dictionary of Word Origins. London: Bloomsbury.

[2] Alemseged, Z et al. (2002). Hominid Cranium from Homo: Description and Taxonomy of Homo-323-1976-896. Am J Phys Anthropol 117 (2): 103–12.

[3] Venter, C & Collins, F (26 June 2000). Speech. Washington, White House.

[4] Ramachandran, V.S. (June 2000). Mirror Neurons and Imitation Learning as the Driving Force behind 'the great leap forward' in Human Evolution. *Edge 69*.

[5] Blakeslee, S. (2006). Cells that Read Minds. *New York Times*, (January 10).

[6] Goleman, D. (2006). Social Intelligence. London: Random House.

[7] Miller, G. (May 12, 2006). Probing the social brain. Science, Vol. 312. no. 5775, pp. 838-839.

[8] Kehoe, J. (1999). Mind Power. Vancouver: Transcontinental.

[9] Blackmore, S. (1999). The Meme Machine. New York: Oxford University Press.

[10] O'Connor, R.D. (1972). Relative efficacy of modelling, shaping, and the combined procedures for modification of social withdrawal. *Journal of Abnormal Psychology*, 79, 327–334.

[11] Flora, C. (July/August, 2005). The Grandmaster experiment. *Psychology Today*.

[12] Cialdini, R.B. (2001). Influence. MA: Allyn & Bacon.

[13] Bargh, J.A. et al. (1996). Automaticity of social behaviour. *Journal of Personality and Social Psychology*.

[14] Key, W.B. (1973). Subliminal Seduction. Englewood Cliffs, NJ: Prentice-Hall.

[15] Obama, B. (February 16, 2008) Democratic Party Dinner. Wisconsin.

[16] Churchill, W. (June 4, 1940) House of Commons. London.

[17] Johann Wolfgang von Goethe. (2004). The Sorrows of Young Werther. New York: Random House.

[18] Phillips, D.P., & Cartensen, L.L. (1988). The effect of suicide stories on various demographic groups, 1986-1985. Suicide and Life-Threatening Behaviour, 18, 100-114.

[19] Anderson, C.A. et al. (2003). The influence of media violence on youth. *Psychological Science in the Public Interest*, 4(3).

[20] Reagan, R. (1990). An American life. New York: Simon & Schuster.

[21] Catherine Ryan Hyde. (2000). Pay it Forward. New York: Simon & Schuster.

[22] http://www.payitforwardfoundation.org

[23] Keegan, R. W. (March 17, 2008) Can a Film Change the World? *Time Magazine.*

[24] Kaufman, S. B. (December, 2008). Confessions of a Late Bloomer. *Psychology Today.*

[25] Driscoll, R. et al. (1972). Parental interference and romantic love: The Romeo and Juliet effect. *Journal of Personality and Social Psychology*, 24, 1-10.

[26] http://www.darwinawards.com/darwin/darwin2007-05.html

[27] http://en.wikipedia.org/wiki/Memory

[28] Allen, V. (2007). Madeleine campaign 'could have put her life in danger'. *Daily Mail*, (November 7).

[29] Laney, C. et al. (2004). Memory for thematically arousing events. *Memory & Cognition*, 32, 1149–1159.

[30] Kensinger E.A, & Corkin, S. (December 2003) Memory enhancement for emotional words: Are emotional words more vividly remembered than neutral words? *Memory & Cognition*, 32.8, 1169-1180.

[31] Miller, A, (2004). Metaphorically Selling. New York: Chiron.

[32] http://www.franklincovey.com

[33] Landsberger, H.A. (1958). Hawthorne Revisited. Ithaca: Cornel University Press.
[34] Cialdini, R.B. (2001). Influence. MA: Allyn & Bacon.

[35] (March 8, 2006). Beware of dissatisfied customers: they like to blab. Knowledge@ Wharton.

[36] Reis, A & L. (2002). The Fall of Advertising and the Rise of Publicity. New York: HarperCollins.

[37] (2007). Driving word of mouth advocacy amongst business executives. Jack Morton White Paper.

[38] Etcoff, N. (1999). Survival of the Prettiest. London: Abacus.

[39] Giles, H. & Powesland, P.F. (1975). Speech Style and Social Evaluation. London: Academic Press.

[40] (2008). Pricing and the Brain. *The Economist*, (January 17)

[41] (2008). Pricing and the Brain. *The Economist*, (January 17)
[42] Seligman, M. (1991). Learned Optimism. New York: Knopf.

[43] http://www.chickensoup.com/cs.asp?cid=about

[44] Jaret, P.E. (2005). Business plan kit for dummies. NJ: Wiley Publishing.

[45] Seligman, M. (2002). Authentic Happiness. London: Nicholas Brealey.

[46] Miller, A. (2004). Metaphorically Selling. New York: Chiron.

[47] Holden, R. (1993). Laughter, the Best Medicine. London: Thorsons.

~

~

To watch Justin Cohen's
inspirational stories go to:

www.biglittlestories.com

~

To book Justin Cohen for your
next conference or training
session go to:

www.justinpresents.com

~